The
Shetland
Sheepdog

An Owner's Guide To

A HAPPY HEALTHY PET

Howell Book House

Howell Book House

Published by Wiley Publishing, Inc., New York, NY

For general information on our other products and services, please contact our Customer Care Department within the U.S. at 800-762-2974, outside the U.S. at 317-572-3993 or fax 317-572-4002.

Wiley also publishes its books in a variety of electronic formats. Some content that appears in print may not be available in electronic books.

Library of Congress Cataloging-in-Publication data

Merrithew, Cathy.
The Shetland Sheepdog: an owner's guide to happy, healthy pet
p.cm.
Includes bibliographical references
ISBN 0-87605-385-1
1. Shetland Sheepdog.   I. Title.
SF429.S62M47   1995
636.7'37—dc20   95-24703
                                       CIP

Manufactured in the United States of America
10 9 8 7 6

Series Director: Dominique De Vito
Series Assistant Director: Felice Primeau
Book Design: Michele Laseau
Cover Design: Iris Jeromnimon
Illustration: Jeff Yesh
Photography:
    Cver photos: puppy, Cathy Merrithew; adult Judith Strom
    Courtesy of the American Kennel Club: 17, 18, 21
    Joan Balzarini: 96
    Mary Bloom: 34-35, 45, 96, 136, 145
    Paulette Braun/Pets by Paulette: 5, 7, 16, 65, 74, 96
    Buckinghamhill American Cocker Spaniels: 148
    Sian Cox: 134
    Dr. Ian Dunbar: 98, 101, 103, 111, 116-117, 122, 123, 127
    Dan Lyons: 96
    Cathy Merrithew: 47, 129
    Liz Palika: 133
    Janice Raines: 132
    Susan Rezy: 96-97
    Judith Strom: 2-3, 8, 9, 11, 13, 20, 22, 23, 24, 25, 27, 28, 29, 31, 36, 39, 41, 42, 43, 48, 52, 55, 56, 57, 59, 61, 63, 69, 83, 96, 107, 110, 128, 130, 135, 137, 139, 140, 144, 149, 150
    Kerrin Winter/Dale Churchill: 80
Production Team: Troy Barnes, John Carroll, Jama Carter, Kathleen Caulfield, Trudy Coler, Vic Peterson, Terry Sheehan, Marvin Van Tiem, Amy DeAngelis and Kathy Iwasaki

Contents

Welcome

to the

World

of the

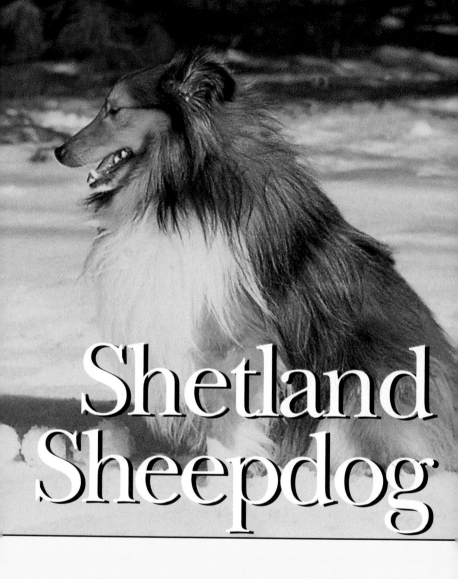

part one

Shetland Sheepdog

External Features of the Shetland Sheepdog

Muzzle

Stop

Cheek

Skull

Shoulder

Crest

Forearm

Neck

Wrist

Withers

Pastern

Dewclaw

Elbow

Back

Loin

Stifle or Knee

Croup

Toes

Hock

chapter 1

What
is a
Shetland
Sheepdog?

Picture this: Out for a walk, you spot a gorgeous, smallish, robust dog, running, leaping and barking, tail wagging. Playing with the neighborhood children, his tongue hanging out, it's obvious they have been at it quite some time. As you approach, he stops playing, fixes his eyes on you and watches. Nonchalantly circling his "flock," he makes sure you are not going to be a threat to him

or his charges. As you draw nearer, you start to admire the dog. He is extremely attractive and it is obvious he has a job to do. As you go past, and glance back over your shoulder, you see that play has resumed, and you go on but never forget that little dog.

You have just met your first Sheltie.

General Appearance

The Shetland Sheepdog truly is a breed of great beauty, intelligence and alertness. Many people refer to them as miniature Collies, and while that may have been true in the early days of the breed, it is not true now. Shetland Sheepdogs are bred true—devoid of any crosses to the Collie or other breeds—and have been for many generations. They are a very manageable, portable size, which suits many families who want a pet they can take anywhere while not taking up too much room. To gain a more complete understanding of the Shetland Sheepdog, we look to the American standard, which describes the Sheltie as "a small, alert, rough-coated, longhaired dog." The general look of the Sheltie should be of a dog that is balanced, slightly longer in body than height, with a proud stance, head held high, not cringing or flattening along the ground. In the following discussion, the sections in italics are taken directly from the American Kennel Club standard; the rest is commentary.

SIZE

Described as a small breed, the dog *should stand between 13 and 16 inches at the shoulder. Note: Height is determined by a line perpendicular to the ground from the top of the shoulder blades. Disqualification—Heights below or above the desired range are to be disqualified from the show ring.*

To properly measure your dog, place it on a hard, level surface. Part and move the hair away from the "highest point of the shoulder blades." Make sure the front legs are straight, with the head in its normal position. Place a ruler or other straight object on the top part of the shoulder blades,

---

WHAT IS A BREED STANDARD?

A breed standard—a detailed description of an individual breed—is meant to portray the *ideal* specimen of that breed. This includes ideal structure, temperament, gait, type—all aspects of the dog. Because the standard describes an ideal specimen, it isn't based on any particular dog. It is a concept against which judges compare actual dogs and breeders strive to produce dogs. At a dog show, the dog that wins is the one that comes closest, in the judge's opinion, to the standard for its breed. Breed standards are written by the breed parent clubs, the national organizations formed to oversee the well-being of the breed. They are voted on and approved by the members of the parent clubs.

making sure it is across, level, and mark the height on a yardstick held next to the front legs. Historically, a Sheltie over sixteen inches was too big and expensive for the founders of the breed to keep and maintain,

and a tiny Sheltie was not able to withstand the rigors of working sheep all day over the rough, uneven terrain. Breeders also questioned whether a tiny herder could properly defend himself or his flock.

Over the years, dogs in the thirteen-to-sixteen-inch height range have best been able to withstand working the countryside. Although dogs under or over the size limit are disqualified from competing toward a championship title, they do not make lesser companions. They may not pass the inspection of a judge, but they will excel as active family pets. Shelties are also high scorers in the obedience ring.

The Sheltie has no problem navigating rough terrain.

COAT

The correct coat *should be double, the outer coat consisting of long, straight, harsh hair; the undercoat short, furry, and so dense as to give the entire coat its "stand off" quality. The hair on the face, tips of ears and feet should be smooth. Mane and frill should be abundant, and particularly impressive in males. The forelegs well feathered, the hind legs less so, but smooth below the hock joint. Hair on tail profuse.*

Without the important outercoat, the coat would become like a sponge, soaking up rain and moisture and preventing the dog from working all day in damp conditions. A full, thick neck ruff is very important because it protects the dog from attackers. Faults are listed as: *Coat short or flat, in whole or in part; wavy, curly, soft or silky. Lack of undercoat. Smooth coated specimens.*

Color: Color is immaterial from a working standpoint, because a good herding dog can be any color. It is said that sheep better distinguish the dog if it is not all white, since that is the sheep's own color. But how can a dog herding all day in bad weather stay its own color anyway? Allowable colors for the show ring are: *sable*, which ranges from golden to red to deep mahogany

with an overlay of black; *tricolor*, which should be an intense black with tan and white markings; *blue merle*, which is a basic background color of silvery blue with black merled throughout and tan markings usually over each eye, along each side of the face and sometimes on the legs and under the tail; *bi-blue*, which is the same as the blue merle but without the tan markings; and *bi-black*, which is the same as the tricolor without tan markings. The bi-black, incidentally, is the original color of the Sheltie, not the sable, as most people commonly believe.

This Sheltie shows an impressive coat.

The current standard penalizes any Sheltie that is more than 50 percent white, although before 1952 "color-headed whites" were allowed to compete in shows. Today, white Collies are allowed to be shown. The color-headed white is, genetically, a sable, black or merle dog on which the white factoring has created a white or spotted body color. They are produced by breeding two dogs carrying the white factoring. The head is always normally colored and marked. The body may be totally white, colored or spotted. All the above colors will have varying amounts of white markings, the most common being around the neck, up each leg, on the face in the form of a blaze or star and on the tip of the tail. White markings are one of the least important parts of a show dog. Full white collars are attractive, but not entirely necessary for a show dog. This is where personal preference enters, because while some people love a lot of white on the blaze, others may like only a pencil-thin stripe up it.

White body spots are considered a fault; however, they do not prevent a herding dog from successfully herding its flock. Brindle is listed as a disqualification, but to my knowledge there has not been a brindle Sheltie for many, many years.

Temperament

Temperament is an extremely important characteristic because, above all else, you must be able to live with your dog and enjoy him. With an average life span of fourteen years, you will want a dog that will be a joy to live with for a long time!

A blue merle in full coat.

The standard states that *the Shetland Sheepdog is an intensely loyal, affectionate dog, and very responsive to its owner. However, it may be reserved toward strangers but not to the point of showing fear or cringing in the ring.* Faults are: *Shyness, timidity, or nervousness. Stubbornness, snappiness, or ill temper.*

Moreover, the Sheltie is self assured and will be concerned when you are upset or not feeling well. A dog with proper temperament will not run up to everyone he meets and jump all over them; rather, he will meet and assess a new person before accepting him or her. This is something the Sheltie has learned in its job herding and protecting its flock.

If you ask anyone about their breed, they will probably tell you that their dog is loyal and affectionate. It would be a rare dog in any breed that would not have these traits. But it is the reference to responsiveness that makes the Shetland Sheepdog stand apart from the rest. The Sheltie will respond quickly to all commands, without question. This takes concentration—something the Sheltie has lots of!

HEAD

Physically, it is the head that epitomizes the Sheltie and sets him apart from the Collie. The sweet and melting expression is what may draw you to the breed, and a proper Sheltie head has a few distinct characteristics.

The head should be refined (not too large to look out of place, and not too tiny to look pointy), *and its shape, when viewed from top or side, be a long blunt wedge tapering slightly from ears to nose, which must be black.* A full underjaw finishes the well-developed head, and it is preferred that the lips meet, with no teeth showing.

The top of the skull should be as flat as possible and the planes should be parallel, with a slight stop just between the eyes. The planes are defined as two parts: the top of the nose, from the top of the nostrils to the corner of the eyes, and right above the eyes to the point at the back of the head, between the ears. Looking from beside your dog, the top line of the top of the head should parallel the top line of the muzzle, but on a higher plane due to the presence of the slight stop. If there were no stop, it would be one level line.

Eyes: *Medium size with dark, almond-shaped rims, set somewhat obliquely in skull. Color must be dark, with blue or merle eyes permissible in blue merles only.* The nose should always be black. The teeth should meet at the front as a scissor bite, with level, evenly spaced teeth. Missing or crooked teeth are considered a fault because they could prevent the dog from defending its flock from attackers. These faults tend to be hereditary, which is important to keep in mind if breeding. Owners should strive for improvement with each generation rather than passing on irreversible faults. If left unchecked, a dog with missing teeth could eventually, a few generations down the road, produce a Sheltie with no teeth!

Ears: *Small and flexible, placed high, carried three-fourths erect, with tips breaking forward. When in repose the ears fold lengthwise and are thrown back into the frill.* The forward tip of the ears is designed to stop rain and snow from entering the ear canal, and keep them free from infections forming due to being wet. The difference between a dog with correct ears and one with prick ears is surprising. A companion dog with prick ears will still make a wonderful pet, and what you choose will come down to personal preference. You will find that your Sheltie's ears can totally change its expression, as ears that are properly trained to tip do make for a sweeter look.

Expression: *Contours and chiseling of the head, the shape, set and use of ears, the placement, shape and color of the eyes, combine to produce expression. Normally the expression should be alert, gentle, intelligent and questioning. Toward strangers the eyes should show watchfulness and reserve, but no fear.*

Even at rest, Shelties remain alert.

Your dog will, and should, be suspicious of strangers. In the early development of the breed, it was not uncommon for good herding dogs to be stolen and resold. Because of its sensitivity, the Sheltie will often read his master's body language and moods, and decide whether or not to accept a stranger on this alone. Shelties seem to have an uncanny knack for sensing when something is wrong, providing them with an intensely strong awareness to guard and protect both master and property. They are also endowed with a strong sense of responsibility. These traits help make the Sheltie an excellent watch dog.

Neck: *Neck should be muscular, arched, and of sufficient length to carry the head proudly.* There must be a nice length of neck to enable the dog to reach forward to prompt its stock to move on. Too short a neck would not allow this important herding feature, which relies on flexibility. Short neck muscles will not have the power of long ones, as a short-necked dog cannot possibly have the forward reach needed for an easy-moving trot. The neck should not be ewed, which some people think looks elegant, but is actually a weakness.

BODY

In overall appearance the body should appear moderately long as measured from shoulder joint to ischium (rearmost extremity of the pelvic bone), but much of this length is actually due to the proper angulation and breadth of the shoulder and hindquarter, as the back itself should be comparatively short. Back should be level and strongly muscled. Chest should be deep, the brisket reaching to the point of the elbow. The ribs should be well sprung, but flattened at their lower half to allow free play of the foreleg and shoulder. Abdomen moderately tucked up.

Lacking in some show dogs today is condition. Remembering its job, a Sheltie needs to be presented in good, hard, working condition. Too many exhibits are entered without any muscle tone at all, leading a judge to speculate that the dog may never be given the chance for proper exercise.

The front legs should be slightly set under the body, and should not appear as straight as a "Terrier" front. The bone must be strong, and muscular, with strong pasterns, with enough bend to provide spring and to help cushion the shock of repeated steps or jumps. The dog's front supports about 70 percent of its weight. A well-angulated front will absorb concussion, help propel the dog on turns, offset lateral displacement and help maintain its center of gravity. As a matter of interest, the shoulder blade is not attached to the spinal column but is held in place by muscles and tendons.

Forequarters: *From the withers the shoulder blades should slope at a 45 degree angle forward and downward to the shoulder joints. At the withers they are separated only by the vertebra, but they must slope outward sufficiently to accommodate the desired spring of the rib. The upper arm should join the shoulder blade at as nearly as possible a right angle. Elbow joint should be equidistant from the ground or from the withers. Forelegs straight, viewed from all angles, muscular and clean, and of strong bone.*

A perfect profile!

Feet (front and hind): *Feet should be oval and compact with toes well arched and fitting tightly together. Pads deep and tough, nails hard and strong.* Feet must be properly constructed. They should point straight ahead and all legs should be straight—no bowing in or out. A weak or splayed foot will break down, eventually, in the working dog. Nails should be watched and trimmed when needed; long nails are definitely a hindrance.

Tail: *The tail should be sufficiently long so that when it is laid along the back edge of the hind legs, the last vertebra will reach the hock joint. Carriage of the tail at rest is straight down or in a slight upward curve. When the dog is alert the tail is normally lifted, but it should not be curved forward over the back.*

A too-short tail may impair your dog's ability to balance. All you need to do is watch your dog running around the yard chasing something. Take note of how his tail whirls around when he wants to slow down. The tail can literally help turn your dog in an instant. It seems to be able to help propel him, too!

GAIT

As the Sheltie is a working dog, it is imperative that the gait be as effortless as possible, with no wasted motion. *The trotting gait of the Shetland Sheepdog should denote effortless speed and smoothness. There should be no jerkiness, nor stiff, up-and-down movement. The drive should be from the rear, true and straight, dependent upon correct angulation, musculation and ligamentation of the entire hindquarter, thus allowing the dog to reach well under its body with its hind foot and propel itself forward. Reach of stride of the foreleg is dependent upon correct angulation, musculation and ligamentation of the forequarters, together with correct width of the chest and construction of rib cage. The foot should be lifted only enough to clear the ground as the leg swings forward. Viewed from the front, both forelegs and hind legs should move forward almost perpendicular to the ground at the walk, slanting a little inward at a slow trot, until at a swift trot the feet are brought so far inward toward center line of body that the tracks left to show two parallel lines of footprints actually touching a center line at their inner edges. There should be no crossing of the feet nor throwing of the weight from side to side.*

The Sheltie must be able to stop and start quickly, and to change direction in an instant. Imagine the dog working all day over all kinds of rough terrain, uneven and difficult footing. Any deviation from a smooth, even gait would in time wear the dog down, and have him do extra motions when not necessary.

An easy way to see if your dog single-tracks is to have him run through a puddle, then down the pavement. See if the footprints come close to each other, touch, cross over or aren't even close! This is why, when watching at a dog show, the judge seems to put so much emphasis on how the dogs run. This is what will show the faults more clearly than having the dog just stand there.

Although a prancing gait seems to many to be correct (and cute!), it is not correct. This usually means the dog is straight in the shoulder and narrow, with no reach and drive.

As an interesting note, many judges today fear that the Sheltie may be headed into trouble because some breeders put too much emphasis on head qualities only. Many seem to forget the Sheltie herds sheep with legs and a body, too—not just with its head! Far too many judges reward dogs with ribbons and points toward their titles just for standing there and looking "pretty," almost closing their eyes to how the dog actually gets around the ring. We should hope the breeder of today and of tomorrow will begin to realize this problem and do something to save this precious little guardian of the flocks and our hearts! Responsible breeders consider both physical and mental soundness the foundation of our breed.

chapter 2

The Shetland Sheepdog's Ancestry

There are as many tales of how the breed came about as there are people to tell these stories. And although the true origins of the breed may never be known with certainty, knowing where the breed originated and why it was developed will help you understand why, in the breed standard, certain traits are desired.

The Shetland Islands

In the foreground of an 1840 engraving showing the town of Lerwick, the capital of the Shetland Islands, is a dog similar in type to the Sheltie, although shorter in height and longer in body. Clearly, one of the forerunners of our modern Sheltie.

It is believed that some type of working Collie was initially brought to the Shetland Islands by fishing fleets of Norway, Sweden, Denmark, Scotland and other northern European countries. When the

Greenland whalers stopped at Shetland to pick up or drop off members of their crews, they brought with them their "Yakkie" dogs (Greenland natives were known among the whalers as the "yaks"). These dogs

crossed with Island dogs, and it is from them, some believe, that we get the smutty (dirty-colored) muzzles and prick ears on some dogs today.

Developed in the Shetland Islands of Scotland, the Shetland Sheepdog's size is no mistake. It has been carefully and selectively bred to be the size it is today. The Shetland Islands are a group of approximately 100 actual islands

"Topaz of Longleigh's," 1938.

and another 100 small land masses. They stretch north from a point about 130 miles north of the northernmost coast of the Scottish mainland. A small percentage of them are actually inhabited, and the others are used to pasture ponies, cattle and sheep. The islands are poor, and have had increasingly difficult economic problems since 1925. Sheep raising has diminished, and has tended to show fewer profits. The inhabitants needed to make a living from the sea and land. It was important to keep the dogs small.

Food and income have never been plentiful. People on the islands raise ponies rather than horses and have become known for their small cattle and, of course, Shetland sheep. It is only natural that the stock dog be diminutive as well! The Shetland Sheepdog is an economical, successful little herding dog, and was always the local shepherd's choice of dog. The shepherds really did not care what their herding dogs looked like, only what they could do. They needed to be tough, courageous, eager, smart and have a coat designed for the job. The coat needed to protect the dog from all elements, including excessive wetness and extreme temperatures. Originally there was no breed standard, so the first Shelties were tremendously different in type. This is why it was, and still is, difficult to know with any certainty the end results of each breeding as far as, for example, type or size.

Most islanders lived on a croft (a township or small farm), and the Sheltie was nicknamed "Toonie," from the Norwegian *tun,* which meant "farm." The dog's job was to keep his flock of sheep from straying off their own small piece of land. The dog was adored as a family pet, and there are tales of the Sheltie as a baby-sitter. They were also affectionately nicknamed "Peerie" dogs, after becoming known as the "fairy" (meaning little) Collies.

"Bil-Bo-Dot Aladdin," 1940.

Members of the Royal Navy who visited the Islands during World War I did much to popularize the breed in Britain. The sailors were attracted to the fluffy little dog, and breeders are said to have sold many puppies to the crew members, who returned to England with them as pets.

A Breed Standardized

In 1908, a meeting was called in Lerwick in an attempt to safeguard the breed. There, the Shetland Collie Club was formed, and the first standard was drawn up. In 1909 recognition was turned down by the Kennel Club. Instead, the Scottish Shetland Sheepdog Club was formed in this same year, producing its own stud book. They were able to publish their own standard, which was not an ideal situation.

In 1908 the standard read: "The type of the Shetland Collie shall be similar to that of the Rough Collie in miniature—the height shall not exceed 15 inches." Only one year later the newly formed Scottish club said: "Appearance: that of the ordinary Collie in miniature: height about 12 inches, weight 10 to 14 pounds." The first standard drawn up by this club gave the points exactly for the Collie, even allowing a "Rough" and a "Smooth." The attempt to produce a smooth-coated Sheltie was abandoned. Since 1941 there has been no such thing as a smooth-coated Sheltie. Four years later, the standard height was altered to read "12 inches is the ideal."

You can see that Shelties around 1910 appeared in the form of very small, Collie-type crosses. Many of the original makers of the breed never wanted the Sheltie to really be a Collie in miniature. The standard said "resemble," not be one!

There were forty-eight Shetland Sheepdogs registered in 1910, and the breed received official recognition in 1914. The breed was listed in the Miscellaneous class along with such other breeds as the Cairn Terrier, Welsh Cockers and Maltese Poodles, to name a few. It was then that the name changed from Shetland Collie to Shetland Sheepdog.

Breeds believed to be behind the Sheltie as we know it today include the Greenland Yakki dogs, Border Collies, the King Charles Spaniel and the Welsh and Scotch Collies. It is from the King Charles we see ticking (which is not a fault and can really be attractive!) on the face, legs and feet, some domed skulls, round eyes and low heavy ears. Some say there must have been some input from the Pomeranian or Spitz breeds, because of the curled tails, prick ears and light bone seen today in some dogs, even in the best of lines.

WHERE DID DOGS COME FROM?

It can be argued that dogs were right there at man's side from the beginning of time. As soon as human beings began to document their existence, the dog was among their drawings and inscriptions. Dogs were not just friends, they served a purpose: There were dogs to hunt birds, pull sleds, herd sheep, burrow after rats—even sit in laps! What your dog was originally bred to do influences the way it behaves. The American Kennel Club recognizes over 140 breeds, and there are hundreds more distinct breeds around the world. To make sense of the breeds, they are grouped according to their size or function. The AKC has seven groups:

1) Sporting, 2) Working,
3) Herding, 4) Hounds,
5) Terriers, 6) Toys,
7) Nonsporting

Can you name a breed from each group? Here's some help: (1) Golden Retriever; (2) Doberman Pinscher; (3) Collie; (4) Beagle; (5) Scottish Terrier; (6) Maltese; and (7) Dalmatian. All modern domestic dogs (*Canis familiaris*) are related, however different they look, and are all descended from *Canis lupus*, the gray wolf.

The Shetland Sheepdog in America

It is believed that the first Sheltie came to the United States around 1910. It may be possible that many

Sheltie owners immigrated into Canada rather than the United States, and it's possible the Sheltie first arrived in Canada. John G. Sherman, Jr., of New York was the first to import registered dogs. It has been documented that the first two imported were dogs by the name of Lord Scott, a pure golden sable whelped February 11, 1905, and Lerwick Bess, a sable and white bitch whelped September 8, 1908. These two dogs were bred by

Handler has her Shetland Sheepdog drop during training.

Sherman, and from this litter came Shetland Rose; all three were registered in 1911.

In 1912 eight dogs were registered, and four of these were direct imports. This was the first year Shelties were exhibited at the prestigious Westminster Kennel

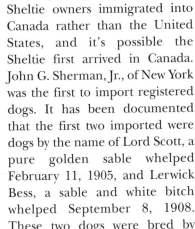

Club dog show in New York. Lerwick Rex became the first Sheltie Champion in the United States, winning his title in 1915. He was, by far, the most famous of the dogs of 1912. Imported by Mr. Sherman, he was by Berry out of Bee, and was bred by Mr. Henderson of Lerwick, Scotland. Whelped March 26, 1910, he was a bi-black (black and white). It would be twelve years before a second Shetland Sheepdog fin-

Handler works her Sheltie on sheep.

ished the requirements of Champion. This was Farburn Captain, owned by Catherine Coleman.

In 1916 Daisy was the only dog being shown in the United States. Breeding and importing had ceased because of the war, and it would be six years before interest in the breed was revived. In 1935 the number of Sheltie registrations totaled 120. By 1942 there were 456, making the Sheltie the twenty-eighth most popular dog. In 1993 the number of Shelties registered with the AKC was 41,113. This makes them the tenth most popular breed in the United States.

By 1923 Sheltie activities were renewed. Registrations this year totaled 258. Of the 19 champions recorded with the club, most of them showed one or another unregistered parent. In February of 1929, the American Shetland Sheepdog Association (ASSA) was formed, held in a dressing room of the original Madison Square Garden, with less than thirty people attending. The ASSA is still very active today, with a membership of over 900. Their first National Specialty was held in May 1933 in conjunction with the Morris and Essex show, and purposely held at a time when Shelties are usually in good coat. With an entry of 15 dogs and 18 bitches, the Best of Breed was CH. Piccolo O'Pages Hill owned by W. W. Gallagher.

An early Sheltie competitor.

The ASSA's annual National shows are still extremely popular. They are held in a different region each year, and it is not unusual for total entries to reach 800 or 900! To continue to educate breeders, these week-long events usually include seminars on various subjects, from reproduction to training to medical problems. Every serious student of the breed should make an effort to attend as many Nationals as possible.

History was made in the American show ring in 1932, when a Sheltie placed in the group for the first time at the Westminster Kennel Club show. This famous dog was Champion Wee Laird O'Downfield, owned by Mrs.

William F. Dreer. Champion Mowgli, son of Wee Laird, was the first American bred Sheltie to attain his Championship. He was owned by Mr. Gallagher, of Page's Hill Sheltie fame. America's first blue merle Champion was Sheltieland Thistle, owned by Catherine Coleman.

Teaching a puppy to sit.

In the British showring of the 1930s it was important for the Shelties to be pretty, and a lot of emphasis was placed on the head and expression. The standard of England and Scotland in 1930 gave a total of 30 points for the head features, almost one third of the total dog. These still are ranked high by the judges of today!

A Famous Sheltie

Although we are all too familiar with "Lassie's" claim to fame from TV, how many remember the Walt Disney TV movie of 1973 titled *The Little Shepherd Dog of Catalina Island* ? Featuring a Champion Sheltie named Birkie, the story finds him lost on Catalina Island. He comes upon a farm, discovers his natural herding abilities and is taken in by the farm owner. The farm's assistant manager fine-tunes his training, and they become close. Birkie's owner, who lives in California, eventually learns of his whereabouts, and when he arrives to retrieve him, Birkie is involved in the rescuing of an Arabian stallion who is about to fall to his death from a cliff. The owner makes the difficult decision to leave Birkie on the farm, where he is retired to stud at the ranch, with his original owner sending other bitches to him for breeding.

Birkie's real name is Gaywyn Sandstorm, Shane for short. He was owned by Carol Snip of St. Louis, Missouri. Shane's film training took seven months. During the film, there were actually four Shelties used.

Shane was used in all close-ups, stills, climbing and running in the field scenes and some of the tricks. Piper, Banner and Cookie were used in some of the herding and chasing scenes. Banner had been trained to attack any animal that the trainers needed him to. I remember watching this great movie, and it is undeniable that these four Shelties did a lot to alert the public about the Shetland Sheepdog!

There is a very active group of people today interested in preserving the Sheltie's ability to herd. Many herding clubs in the United States and Canada have been quite successful writing rules and regulations for herding trials, and many have already successfully acquired a title or degree in this sport.

There are many attributes that go into the making of a good stock dog. They must display an instinct to herd, which involves more than simply being interested in the livestock and the natural ability to round them up and control them. Training will encourage the instinct, but it will not create it. Herding is a sport that will get increasingly popular, and we will definitely see more Shelties in this competitive field in the future.

This versatile Sheltie does a retrieve in open obedience.

In 1956 a Sheltie was awarded the coveted Ken-L-Ration Dog Hero award after barking and pulling at the sheets, waking his owners, to warn them that their son was bleeding following a tonsillectomy.

chapter 3

The **World**
According to the
Shetland
Sheepdog

Just check the show and trial results of any club, and you will notice one breed in particular at the top of the winner's podium in almost any event. The Shetland Sheepdog. This is one handy little dog! Game for anything you ask of it, your Sheltie will work with you on any project, or against you if there's something of which he is unsure. Plain and simple, this dog is good at everything he does. What attracts a lot of

people to the Sheltie is his versatility. The Sheltie's steady growth in popularity is, in part, due to his talent of adapting to most any situation. The Sheltie is adored for his willingness to please, whether as a full-time companion, a work partner (one that accompanies his owner to work) or a competition dog.

Most Shelties do have a workaholic nature, which obviously makes them one of the most popular obedience dogs. Only few show a strong retrieving instinct, which may make the dumbbell work difficult to teach, but once they are shown what is expected, they never look back!

Shelties are sometimes described as being catlike in their household manners. Extremely clean and equally easy to housebreak, they are usually never destructive in the home. Properly brought up and given fair house manners, they are clean, tidy dogs. They can even be taught to put their toys away in a toybox after playing with them!

The Sheltie is Versatile

Your dog can show in conformation shows and earn enough points to achieve the coveted title of Champion, compete successfully in obedience, and earn the titles of CD (Companion Dog), CDX (Companion Dog Excellent), UD (Utility Dog) or the newest title available to obedience enthusiasts, UDX (Utility Dog Excellent). For those who like the great outdoors, tracking is a wonderful sport, with the titles TD (Tracking Dog) or TDX (Tracking Dog Excellent) available. Agility, which is a fast-moving and equally fast-growing sport of timed obstacle course racing, requires not only your dog to be physically fit, but you, too. Titles are also awarded for successful wins in this field, including NAD (Novice Agility Dog), OAD (Open Agility Dog), ADX (Agility Excellent) and MAX (Master Agility). There is flyball, a timed relay race consisting of a team of four dogs jumping hurdles one dog at a time, releasing a ball

Moving ducks in a herding test.

from a box, catching it and racing back over the hurdles with the ball. Titles to be won are FD (Flyball Dog), FDX (Flyball Dog Excellent) and FDCH (Flyball Dog Champion). In herding, titles are HT (Herding Tested), PT (Pre-Trial Tested), HS, HI, HX (Herding Started, Herding Intermediate, Herding Excellent), and H.Ch. (Herding Champion). Musical freestyle has the dog, along with the owner, performing a routine of modified obedience exercises choreographed to music. Scent hurdling is quite popular—another timed event with a team of four dogs jumping hurdles singly and retrieving a dumbbell, which their owner has "scented" with their own scent, from a platform with the other dogs' dumbbells. The trick here is for the dog to pick the one its owner has touched.

For those who would like to volunteer at their local hospitals or extended care unit, pet therapy or hospital visitations are very exciting. This is a fantastic way to brighten someone's life.

For younger dog enthusiasts, junior handling is a very competitive sport, where the junior is judged on his or her ability to best present their dog to the judge—not on the merits of the dog.

Another job the Sheltie excels at is as a hearing ear dog. These are dogs (not always specifically Shelties) specially trained to be the ears of deaf or almost deaf people. They will alert their owner to the doorbell, phone, smoke detector,

A DOG'S SENSES

Sight: With their eyes located further apart than ours, dogs can detect movement at a greater distance than we can, but they can't see as well up close. They can also see better in less light, but they can't distinguish many colors.

Sound: Dogs can hear about four times better than we can, and they can hear high-pitched sounds especially well. Their ancestors, the wolves, howled to let other wolves know where they were; our dogs do the same, but they have a wider range of vocalizations, including barks, whimpers, moans and whines.

Smell: A dog's nose is his greatest sensory organ. His sense of smell is so great he can follow a trail that's weeks old, detect odors diluted to one-millionth the concentration we'd need to notice them, even sniff out a person under water!

Taste: Dogs have fewer taste buds than we do, so they're likelier to try anything—and usually do, which is why it's especially important for their owners to monitor their food intake. Dogs are omnivores, which means they eat meat as well as vegetable matter like grasses and weeds.

Touch: Dogs are social animals and love to be petted, groomed and played with.

baby crying, kettle boiling—the list goes on and on. Shelties are naturals at this, and many are being used today for this purpose. They are trained to go to the owner and jump on them, or turn and run at the door, etc., to alert the owner that something is happening.

Last but not least, there's just plain loving that Sheltie!

REX

Hang gliding has been taken up by at least one dog of which I know. Rex is owned by Kim Cooper of Orleans, Ontario, Canada. She wrote to me and filled me in on her sky dog. She writes:

Rex is no show dog. He's just a typical Sheltie, with the heart of a big dog in a little dog's body and an I.Q. that Lassie would envy. Rex and I are the best of friends—we do everything together. He mastered obedience to the UD level by the age of two, so we moved on. He loved flyball and did well at tracking and search and rescue. About the only thing we didn't try our hand at was Schutzhund!

Rex and I camp together all summer long. He's got his own backpack, as I insist

A 3-month-old puppy gets used to her new family.

that he carry the kibble when we hike off into the woods. He can carry a full seven-day supply without a second thought. Last summer, he completed the 120 km Tour de Mont Blanc, covering nine mountain passes over 2,500 meters high. That's no mean feat for any dog, let alone a toy breed. He's proof positive that Shelties truly are working dogs.

Rex is also a hang glider pilot—well, passenger anyway. When I took up the sport, Rex indicated that he wanted to fly too, by chasing me off the edge of a couple of cliffs. In the interests of his health, I rigged a harness for him and took him up. After the first few moments of surprise at floating over the Earth, he settled down

to enjoy the ride. I can't see him when we fly, but spectators tell me he's got his nose in the wind and a smile on his face. He loves barking at passing birds. He's shown some distaste for crash landings but that's understandable. I'm not keen on them myself!

A tricolor picks up a Frisbee.

Rex has shown me that Shelties are one of the most versatile dogs going. All he asks is to be included in my life and to be challenged. In return, I have a faithful and fun companion. Now that's a fair trade if I've ever seen one.

Kim, I think that fully describes our breed!

Eating comes naturally to them—meaning it is rare to have a Sheltie that won't eat. The exception to this is one that has taught her owner to let her be picky, but as a rule, they will eat anything put in front of them!

The Sheltie's tendency to bark is one of its downsides. This can be a problem, so I always warn prospective buyers about the breed's affinity for barking. Of course, this makes the Sheltie a great watchdog—it will not let much go by without letting you know. Depending on what you want from your dog, this may or may not be a problem.

In this day and age, with neighbors getting closer and closer, I caution everyone about staying friendly with their neighbor and keeping the dog from incessant barking. Most towns have a noise bylaw, with dog barking one of the things for which you can be fined, if it happens during certain hours of the day or night. Do not put your neighbor in the position of having to complain to the city or town about your dog barking. You will need to stay on good terms with them!

For those who cannot break their dog from barking, there is a surgical procedure called de-barking available. Usually done as a last resort, it is an option when persistent barking means either having to part with your dog or getting into trouble with the city laws. I have had this procedure done on a few of my dogs, and they don't even know they can't bark. Please speak with your veterinarian about this procedure and do it if necessary.

Please keep in mind that a dog will always bark for a reason. It may be because there is someone approaching your house, yard or car. If your dog barks during the night, find out why. Maybe your dog is alerting you to a prowler or smoke. The number one reason dogs bark when outside is boredom. If you leave your dog in the backyard, he will bark when there's nothing to do. Remedy this by giving your Sheltie some safe toys, going for a walk, playing ball. Don't let your dog become bored and bother the neighborhood.

The Sheltie is Active

Some people find the Sheltie altogether too active. They may not be the best breed for an elderly couple who cannot give them the exercise they need.

Shelties truly think they are a part of the family.

Sometimes a good exercise program can be simply throwing a tennis ball in the yard. If you take your Sheltie to a park (one that allows dogs, of course) and hit the tennis ball with a racquet, she will play for a long time and basically run until she drops—fantastic exercise!

A lot of Shelties tend to do everything at top speed. This includes going for walks, leaping into the car (they love to go everywhere with you), playing ball, answering the phone with you (chasing you), and herding the kids! Certain dogs love nothing better than to be playing with a group of kids, circling them at a distance and kind of keeping them all together. It's wonderful when you see this in action, and many people wouldn't even notice.

CHARACTERISTICS OF THE SHETLAND SHEEPDOG

Little or no hunting instinct

Good with children

Willing to live with other animals

Lives to guard its flock (translation: you, your family and home)

No desire to roam

Barks

Sheds

Happy living outside or inside

Shelties are neither delicate nor fragile. If anything, for their size they are one of the toughest, hardiest breeds. Although they rarely need much physical correction, they will accept it, feeling that as the owner, you must be right. They will almost never challenge their owner during a correction. Voice corrections are usually the only type of punishment needed—often more effective than a scruff-shake or roll.

I am asked regularly which sex makes a better pet. I have to answer that I have no preference. I feel this is one breed where males and females are equally well suited to be pets. Assuming you will have your Sheltie spayed or neutered, the only difference may be in the amount of coat or adult size. Males typically have more coat than females. Although Shelties are usually not dog aggressive, some are. Neutering will definitely extinguish this dangerous act.

The Sheltie has an incredible desire to obey its owner. They are also guilty of putting their trust in you, and rely on you not to let them down. If you give your Sheltie the chance, he will literally love you to death, and will be hoping for the same in return from you! Your love means more to your dog than expensive toys or premium food. Dogs are social animals and want very much to be a part of your family. Raise them

Shelties guard their family members as if they were part of their flock.

fairly and with consistency. Make sure everyone in the family keeps him off the couch, if that's one of your rules, along with no begging at the table or jumping up on people. It is not fair to expect your dog to know who allows certain things and who does not. Add to this to your understanding and appreciation of your dog, and you will have probably the best dog in the world!

MORE INFORMATION ON SHETLAND SHEEPDOGS

NATIONAL BREED CLUB

American Shetland Sheepdog Association
Mr. George Page, Corresponding Secretary
1100 Cataway Place
Bryans Road, MD 20616

The club can give you information on all aspects of the breed, including the names and addresses of breed, obedience and herding clubs in your area. Inquire about membership.

BOOKS

Davis, Mary. *Pet Owner's Guide to the Shetland Sheepdog.* New York: Howell Book House, 1993.

Nicholas, Anna Katherine. *The Book of the Shetland Sheepdog.* Neptune, N.J.: TFH Publications, 1979.

Riddle, Maxwell. *The New Complete Shetland Sheepdog.* New York: Howell Book House, 1992.

Ross, Barb. *The Illustrated Guide to Sheltie Grooming.* Loveland, Colo.: Alpine Publications, 1993.

Sucher, Jamie. *Shetland Sheepdogs, A Complete Pet Owner's Manual.* Hauppauge, N.Y.: Barron's Educational Series, 1990.

Taggart, Mari. *Sheepdog Training, an All-Breed Approach.* Loveland, Colo.: Alpine Publications, 1991.

MAGAZINES

Sheltie Advantage, 5765 Woodwall Street, Detroit, MI 48224.

Sheltie Pacesetter, P.O. Box 158, McKenzie, TN 38201.

Sheltie International, P.O. Box 6369, Los Osos, CA 93412.

VIDEOS

American Kennel Club. *Shetland Sheepdogs.*

Living

with a

part two

Shetland Sheepdog

chapter 4

Bringing your
Shetland Sheepdog
Home

Everyone loves puppies. But not everyone can handle the responsibility that puppies require. Hopefully, you have given thought to whether or not the Sheltie will fit into your lifestyle and you've looked in to what it will cost for upkeep. You have decided you have the spare time necessary to look after the Sheltie's grooming needs and the necessary energy to devote to housebreaking and training. Your budget is telling you that you can spend the money on the items you'll need before and after you find your perfect puppy. Basically, all dogs cost about the same to buy. Overall, vaccinations cost the same for all sizes of dogs, registration costs the same, and so on. As a rule, Shelties can be a low-upkeep breed.

This chapter will outline a few important steps to take to ensure that you raise the happiest and healthiest Sheltie possible.

Puppy Proofing

Before you bring your puppy home, be sure to puppy-proof your house. Just like babies, puppies will pick up anything and put it in their mouths. Make sure electrical cords are stashed out of puppy's way. Try wrapping the cord with aluminum foil. That will be slightly uncomfortable for your puppy to chew. Gather up all excess cord and twist-tie it together. Hide it behind curtains or tack it to the back of the couch. You can get quite inventive if you want. Watch especially at Christmas time if you have a young puppy. Christmas-tree light cords can easily electrocute a puppy if not supervised.

Make sure your garbage container is hidden away in a closable cupboard or up on the counter. Puppies love to tip garbage cans over in the search for good-tasting morsels. Many poisonings are linked to owner negligence. Keep all poisonous substances out of your puppy's reach.

Leaving a container of antifreeze where your puppy can get into it is deadly because the active ingredient, ethylene glycol, is toxic to dogs. It is attractive to dogs because it is sweet smelling. They may even lap it up from a puddle left in the driveway from a leak. If you notice your dog licking up even just a tiny amount of antifreeze, get it to the vet as soon as possible. Signs to look for are lack of coordination, vomiting and depression.

Some owners simply give their dogs aspirin, ibuprofen or acetaminophen. The latter can actually cause liver damage. Ibuprofen is sugar coated, and many dogs would eat a whole bottle. Signs of this poisoning include severe vomiting, stomach ulcerations and kidney damage. Just because you take these medications for pain, do not assume they are okay for use in dogs.

PUPPY ESSENTIALS

Your new puppy will need:

food bowl

water bowl

collar

leash

I. D. tag

bed

crate

toys

grooming supplies

Dogs should be protected from all pesticides, herbicides and fertilizers, both indoor and out. After using any of these on the lawn, be sure to water it and let it dry before letting the dog on it. If your dog shows signs of poisoning, like vomiting, depression or even seizures, call your veterinarian immediately. Depending on what the poison is, without fast and proper action your dog could be dead within minutes. If you know what he has gotten into, keep the container handy so you can inform your veterinarian of the ingredients. If you can, gather up what's left so he or she can tell how much of it your dog may have eaten. See more on poisoning in Chapter 7.

Other attractions to puppies and dogs are fishing line, string, pantyhose, underwear, corncobs, peach pits, kids' toys, small balls and sponges, and any bulb plants that may be in your garden. The list could go on and on—please use common sense when puppy-proofing your home.

Where to Get Your Puppy

How do you go about finding that special dog of which you have been dreaming? Well, you have several options. Look in the newspaper, visit pet stores, contact local veterinarians or boarding kennels, inquire about breeders in the area or get in touch with your local rescue group.

Keep in mind certain things: You want a puppy that will be healthy and bred with care. You must make an educated choice, not just follow your heart and pick the most adorable or first available puppy. A local veterinarian is a good person to talk to when starting your search. Chances are he or she will know who's breeding Shelties in your area and may be able to refer you to someone. The vet can also advise you on what to look for in a puppy: bright eyes; healthy skin and coat; normal activity level; and good temperament (there are even puppy temperament tests you can perform— ask the vet or puppy seller if they know about them).

Your best bet is to find a reliable breeder. As a rule, they want you to be happy with your choice, and because you will have this dog for an average of twelve years, you too want to make the right choice. Dog shows are perfect places to track down breeders. Take

the time to watch the Sheltie judging. If a certain dog appeals to you, approach the owner or handler following the judging. Most likely, these folks will be more than pleased to talk with you and tell you all about their dogs! Or pick up a copy of a dog magazine that has listings of breeders, such as *Dog Fancy* or *Dog World*. A reputable breeder usually sells the puppy with a lifetime commitment to answer any questions you may have, and advise you if problems come up. He or

A ten-week-old puppy is already a good retriever!

she will truly want each pup to live a long, healthy life with their special owner. Most breeders sell on a guarantee, with clear instructions to what they will do for you—the buyer. Remember—don't impulse-buy. Visit as many kennels as you can and take notes. Be sure to call ahead and schedule a time to visit to ensure that the breeder will be able to take the time to sit down with you and discuss the breed. Don't be fooled into thinking that there are no hereditary problems in the breed. There definitely are.

Find a breeder who does health checks on their breeding stock. Do not buy from a breeder who insists their line is free of inherited problems yet cannot produce documentation to prove it. This should include yearly eye clearances, hip dysplasia X raying, blood tests to rule out defects such as Von Willebrand's and thyroid problems, to name a few. They will have documentation, so don't let them simply tell you the dogs are clear—they should be able to provide either original documents or photocopies.

After you've chosen your ideal breeder, expect to wait for a litter if there are no puppies available. Be patient. You've done your homework, and hopefully you've found the breeder who will keep in touch with you after the sale is made. The reputable breeder will want to keep in touch and see how puppy is maturing, as they are always striving to better each breeding, and will learn something from every litter they have.

You may wish to contact a Sheltie club and inquire about adopting a rescue dog. These are Shelties that for whatever reason have been discarded by their owners, or are hopelessly lost with no way to trace them. They are adopted by a caring member of the breed club. These wonderful folks clean them up, groom them, see to it they are checked by a veterinarian and set out to place them in a new home. This is a thoughtful act by someone who wants to give a dog a second chance.

Coming Home

Christmas, birthdays and other special occasion days are not the best time to introduce a puppy into the household. Especially if they are surprise gifts! These times are usually hectic, and the puppy gets forgotten and confused trying to fit in.

Things to take when you pick up your puppy include: paper towels (in case of any car sickness on the way home), a crate (to safely travel home in) and plastic

---

HOUSEHOLD DANGERS

Curious puppies and inquisitive dogs get into trouble not because they are bad, but simply because they want to investigate the world around them. It's our job to protect our dogs from harmful substances, like the following:

IN THE HOUSE

cleaners, especially pine oil

perfumes, colognes, aftershaves

medications, vitamins

office and craft supplies

electric cords

chicken or turkey bones

chocolate

some house and garden plants, like ivy, oleander and poinsettia

IN THE GARAGE

antifreeze

garden supplies, like snail and slug bait, pesticides, fertilizers, mouse and rat poisons bags to put any used paper towels in. So you're on your way home with your new puppy sitting somewhat excitedly in your lap (as long as you're not driving!) or resting nicely in the crate. Puppy is riding happily along, inquisitive about the things zipping by outside.

Now what will you do with your new Sheltie when you arrive home? Hopefully you have already built a secure, doggy-proof fence. A chain-link fence is the best, but solid wood is great, too. Make sure the latch on the gate cannot be opened easily by your Sheltie's nose; some latches are not dog proof. You may also want to consider invis-

ible fencing, although this does not prevent loose dogs from wandering onto your property.

A new puppy will feel safe and secure in his crate.

Basic Supplies

If you don't already have one, this is the time to purchase a crate. This will become puppy's "home away from home," or "den." It will prevent your puppy from doing a lot of expensive damage, like chewing your shoes or couch, urinating on the rug, chewing light cords—which can be deadly—basically, just plain damage. Any pet store will have them, or watch the newspapers or garage sales for used ones. You may prefer to have your dog stay on her own bed, which is fine, too, and will also take some training time. Every time you want your Sheltie to go to her bed, actually say "bed" and point it out. And always remember, for proper actions it's usually best if the bed stays in the same place; in a corner or under a desk is good, as it is like a den area.

You will need a bowl for food and water. Make sure you find out from your breeder what kind of food puppy is being fed and pick some up before you get the puppy.

Cheaper food will increase the amount of stool your puppy produces, which can make housebreaking harder and more work for you. Talk to the staff at the pet store, and remember you usually get what you pay for. If your puppy comes from a different town, carry a bottle so you can take some water from your breeder's home. Some puppies will get dietary upsets if their water is changed abruptly. Mix a bit of the old and new water together for about a week or so and puppy will adjust fine. If you forget, pick up a bottle of drinking water at the corner store and use it instead.

Buy a lightweight buckle collar, or one of the snap-on collars. *Never* use choke chains on young puppies. These can and will choke your dog. They are training tools only, and should *never* be left on a dog with you not there.

To get your puppy used to a buckle collar, fasten it on while you are playing. Keep it on for a while, allowing your puppy to scratch at it and get used to it. Take it off when you're finished playing. When your puppy is no longer bothered by it, attach a lead, letting it hang. It will catch on things and your puppy will have to stop and figure it out and see it's nothing to worry about. After that, pick up the lead and put gentle pressure on

It takes time for a young puppy to get accustomed to a collar.

it. Use your voice in a happy tone and ask your puppy to follow you. Food treats are great—give a slight tug, and when you get a positive response, give a treat. One tip— buy an adjustable snap on collar to enable you to make it bigger as your puppy grows. This will prevent you from having to buy several over the course of the years. Try not to get a wide one, as it will flatten the coat too much around the neck and make it harder to comb through. A rolled leather buckle collar or no more than a half inch nylon collar are the best. Invest in a leather leash or nylon; you won't be comfortable using a chain leash. These are heavy, and too hard on your hands. When you enroll in obedience class, chain leads are not allowed.

A good-quality leather lead will no doubt last your dog a lifetime.

The First Checkup

It is always a good idea to schedule a visit to your veterinarian with your new puppy within twenty-four to forty-eight hours after purchase. This will ensure

A crate is the safest place for your Sheltie to ride.

that your puppy is healthy, and if there are any problems, it is much easier to return your puppy this early before you have become too attached. With most breeders, this is part of the sales agreement. They will want you to be assured your new puppy is happy and healthy.

What to Expect from Your Puppy

A typical schedule for a new puppy may go something like this: Sleeps in his crate or bed for the night. You may need to get up once or twice for the first few nights to take your new pal for a walk. You will definitely need to do so as soon as possible. Slip on your shoes and out you go. Stay out until your puppy is finished relieving himself, give lots of praise and go back in. You will want to feed the puppy breakfast, and after eating, you'll need to take him out again. After a successful jaunt, it will be playtime! Your puppy probably will need to nap shortly after—he may even fall asleep sitting up! I recommend putting your new

Sheltie into his crate for a nap. After sleeping for a couple hours or more, you may hear crying, so out you go again! This will be repeated quite a few times in the day, and lunch is usually served at around noon. I feed again around five in the evening, then a light snack at bedtime. I say a light snack here—filling your puppy up before bed is just asking for a trip outside once or twice in the middle of the night! As your puppy gets older, replace the bedtime snack with a dog biscuit.

Whatever schedule you choose, please be fair and keep it as close as possible to the same each day. This will make housebreaking a snap, and will teach a routine which dog's thrive on! A walk around the block once or twice a day will make you look like "God" in your dog's eyes. When he is a young puppy, start out by just going to the end of your driveway, then the next driveway up, and keep increasing the distance over a few days. This will help your puppy get used to cars whizzing by, which can be scary to the puppy that is trying to relate to a new home. You'll be amazed at how quickly your new puppy will recognize her own driveway on the way home. This is one of the very best exercises for dogs. A daily walk, even if it is just around the block, will keep your Sheltie fit and in good muscle tone.

A free run in a dog-friendly park is also terrific exercise. If allowed to run with other dogs, yours will learn how to get along with them, and not be inclined to try to fight when meeting new friends. Be sure your dog knows how to come when called in an instant before doing this. You may need to call your dog back if he is approached by a dog that was not socialized as a youngster and who may want to dominate yours!

I strongly recommend locating a puppy kindergarten class and enrolling your puppy. This will help with socializing, and some inducive (no force) training will get you on your way to a strong bond with your pet. The next level of training will be a continuation from this class, teaching you basic home obedience and control. Check with the local or nearest dog club for dates to sign up.

Puppy Ears

When you bring your puppy home, you will notice that your breeder probably glued her ears over. This trains the ear to tip forward, giving the Sheltie that adorable expression! A lot of bloodlines have naturally tipped ears, meaning that they will tip naturally without any extra help. Other lines need help. If the ear is small and pointy, it may want to go prick—meaning straight up in the air! What we use is a fabric glue, found in most sewing and novelty stores. All you need is a dab of glue on the tip of the ear. With your dog sitting in front of you, or better yet on some-one else's lap so they can steady the head, carefully fold the ear over your little

Her ears have the perfect tip!

finger and stick it to the base of the ear, right where it hooks on the top of the head. Be sure to not fold the ear too sharply or you can cut off the circulation and possibly lose the ear tip! Don't press too hard, just lightly. The glue will stick. Keep hold of your puppy for a few minutes. It will want to shake its head and scratch at the new sensation. If the ear comes up, try again.

You can start this on a puppy as young as seven or eight weeks. You'll want to keep on top of the ears at least until your puppy stops teething, which is usually around nine months of age. When they're teething, the ears will go up, down, one up and one down; the next day they'll reverse, and just when you're about to give up, they'll look exactly right! If an ear comes unglued, and looks like it's tipping nicely, I'll usually let it stay undone for a day or two. If it goes straight up—glue again! I leave the glue on to fall off on its own, but if you want to remove it, try a nonaerosol adhesive remover. There are other ways to help the ears along, but this is the simplest and easiest. If it does not work for you, contact your breeder. If your breeder lives too far away, try calling someone you've met that has Shelties. Chances are they have been through this, too, and most fanciers will be more than happy to assist you.

chapter 5

Feeding
your
Shetland
Sheepdog

Feeding dogs used to be simple. There were few dog foods available until recently. With not many to choose from, it seemed to be easy to make a choice and be happy with it. Now, with so many types and brands from which to choose, it has become a monumental task. And one that is crucial to your Sheltie's health and happiness.

What to Feed

For optimum health, a combination of six classes of nutrients are needed. Water, protein, carbohydrates, fats, minerals and vitamins. To ensure that your Sheltie is getting all of these nutrients, you need look no further than to a commercial dog food. But with so many different kinds on the market, which one should you choose?

Common sense tells us that dogs will benefit more from premium food than they will from cheap food, which tends to be made out of inferior ingredients. Pet stores and your veterinarian's office are the first places to look when choosing a food for your dog.

Federal law requires manufacturers to list the ingredients on each bag or can of food. These labels are a wealth of information. For clarification, animal by-products refer to animal parts that are not used for human consumption. This includes bone meal, liver, lung and kidney.

The first ingredient listed on your dog's food is the one that is the most significant.

Make sure to give your puppy safe chews.

They are listed in descending order of predominance, by weight. Presumably, the ingredient that weighs the most is listed first. Because fresh meat contains water, it is usually the heaviest, so it is listed first. Meat meals are dried, becoming more concentrated forms of protein. The next few ingredients are also important, but the rest probably appear in only small amounts. Unfortunately, this information alone will not ensure that you select the best brand for your dog. Your dog must eat the food in order to reap its benefits. Whatever food you choose, make sure your dog eats it!

Be sure to try a food for a minimum of six to eight weeks before deciding if it is right for your dog. You will not see dramatic improvements in your dog until at least then, if not later. A good test of whether or not the food is benefiting your dog is by stool volume and consistency. You want it to be firm and tight, not loose and runny, as poor-quality protein will pass through a dog's intestinal tract unused. Watch for weight loss or gain.

Performance foods are designed for active dogs—not every dog! They usually do not contain soy, and always contain high-quality ingredients. They have an average of 3 percent crude protein and 2 percent crude fat.

Canned food should not make up the bulk of your dog's diet. If you check the label, you will find the moisture level to be quite high. This means you are paying a lot to feed your dog water. If your dog is partial to moist, rather than dry food, you can mix a few tablespoons of canned food into the dry. Some dogs find this more appealing. Semimoist foods are designed to look appealing to you as well as your dog, but are discouraged because of the high sugar level, and usually food coloring is added to make it look like meat. This is not a good diet for the Sheltie.

WATER

Your dog relies on you to provide a constant supply of fresh, clean water. The bucket or bowl will need to be frequently washed. Water should always be available for your dog!

SUPPLEMENTS

If you are feeding a premium food, you should not need supplements, such as vitamins or coat enhancers. In certain circumstances, however, your Sheltie may need some help in the form of a coat enhancer. Speak with your veterinarian before adding anything, because some supplements can do more harm than good. If the food you have chosen is already completely balanced, additions will cause an imbalance.

STORING DOG FOOD

Storing your dog food is very important. It is best to leave it in the original bag, but

---

HOW MANY MEALS A DAY?

Individual dogs vary in how much they should eat to maintain a desired body weight—not too fat, but not too thin. Puppies need several meals a day, while older dogs may need only one. Determine how much food keeps your adult dog looking and feeling her best. Then decide how many meals you want to feed with that amount. Like us, most dogs love to eat, and offering two meals a day is more enjoyable for them. If you're worried about overfeeding, make sure you measure correctly and abstain from adding tidbits to the meals.

Whether you feed one or two meals, only leave your dog's food out for the amount of time it takes her to eat it—10 minutes, for example. Freefeeding (when food is available any time) and leisurely meals encourage picky eating. Don't worry if your dog doesn't finish all her dinner in the allotted time. She'll learn she should.

be sure to seal it tightly each time you open it. Do not store the food in plastic garbage cans, because it can have a bad effect on the food. Breaking a big bag into a few small containers is good, as it assures each one will be fresh as you use it. Remember that the average shelf life for a bag of dry food can be anywhere from ten months to one year, depending on the preservatives used by different companies.

HOW MUCH?

How much you feed your dog will vary depending on activity level, age, health and the brand of food you choose. A good start is to offer your puppy a handful and a bit more each meal for the adult. Adjust how much you feed based on weight gain or loss. The feeding guidelines on the dog food bag or can will provide you with the recommended daily feeding amounts. Remember that they are guidelines and not necessarily right for every dog!

Special Considerations
DENTAL HEALTH

Feeding a strictly dry food, without adding water, is believed to be beneficial to your dog's teeth. Hard food helps to prevent tartar buildup by providing friction each time your dog chews, therefore removing plaque.

Rawhides are another way to keep dental problems from forming. Remember to always supervise your

---

HOW TO READ THE DOG FOOD LABEL

With so many choices on the market, how can you be sure you are feeding the right food for your dog? The information is all there on the label—if you know what you're looking for.

Look for the nutritional claim right up top. Is the food "100% nutritionally complete"? If so, it's for nearly all life stages; "growth and maintenance," on the other hand, is for early development; puppy foods are marked as such, as are foods for senior dogs.

Ingredients are listed in descending order by weight. The first three or four ingredients will tell you the bulk of what the food contains. Look for the highest-quality ingredients, like meats and grains, to be among them.

The Guaranteed Analysis tells you what levels of protein, fat, fiber and moisture are in the food, in that order. While these numbers are meaningful, they won't tell you much about the quality of the food. Nutritional value is in the dry matter, not the moisture content.

In many ways, seeing is believing. If your dog has bright eyes, a shiny coat, a good appetite and a good energy level, chances are his diet's fine. Your dog's breeder and your veterinarian are good sources of advice if you're still confused.

dog while it is chewing the rawhide because it may try to swallow the last part before it is small enough. Some rawhides are treated with chemicals to preserve them, which can make your dog very sick, so use caution when selecting a brand. Talk to your veterinarian about this and go with his or her advice.

PUPPIES

A puppy will need a premium quality puppy food specifically developed for optimum growth and development. These are higher in proteins, carbohydrates, fats and minerals. I do not recommend the practice of bringing a puppy home, starting it on a baby food/pablum diet because it is not a balanced diet for dogs and you will need to wean your puppy off it and onto puppy food anyway. I start weaning pups around four weeks with the puppy food I plan to use. Soaking it first in hot water, for about ten to fifteen minutes will soften it enough for the puppies to easily eat. Gradually leave it harder until seven to eight weeks, when they are eating it dry. I have never run into a problem feeding puppies this way.

> ### TO SUPPLEMENT OR NOT TO SUPPLEMENT?
>
> If you're feeding your dog a diet that's correct for her developmental stage and she's alert, healthy-looking and neither over- nor underweight, you don't need to add supplements. These include table scraps as well as vitamins and minerals. In fact, a growing puppy is in danger of developing musculoskeletal disorders by oversupplementation. If you have any concerns about the nutritional quality of the food you're feeding, discuss them with your veterinarian.

A puppy will need to eat at least four times a day from the age of weaning (approximately four weeks and up) until four months of age. Between four and six months, you could change to three times a day. I would suggest keeping your puppy's meals on par with yours, with breakfast in the morning, a second meal around noon and a final meal at dinnertime. At bedtime, puppy would appreciate a biscuit when going into her crate to sleep for the night. This will hold your Sheltie's hunger until morning, without filling it up and necessitating a trip outside during the night.

ALLERGIES

Lamb and rice diets are believed to be the most well tolerated and are hailed as being best for dogs with skin afflictions. Even the hypoallergenic diets available from your veterinarian are based on lamb and rice. Veterinarians will caution you not to switch if your dog is not allergic to what you are already feeding him. Instead, feed a high-quality chicken- or beef-based food right from the beginning. If your dog does develop a food allergy, lamb and rice are protein sources that haven't already been a part of your dog's diet. You can gradually add to her diet and rule out possible allergens. Check around, talk to your breeder or veterinarian, then form your own decision.

FOODS TO AVOID

You should avoid giving your Sheltie candies, pastries, foods that are spicy or greasy or bones that splinter, such as chicken, pork chop and steak bones. Your dog could die from the abrasions caused by the splinters traveling through the intestines. Most importantly, you must not give your dog chocolate. It is poisonous to dogs and does not take much to make a dog sick. Theobromine is the active ingredient that dogs cannot tolerate.

Feed your Sheltie dog food—not people food.

Do not be tempted to feed your dog table scraps. They can cause dietary upsets and may induce a serious problem known as pancreatitis, a problem that is not fun for your dog. Fatty meats are often the culprits. As a rule, Shelties are not droolers or beggers, so you should be able to teach your dog to lie quietly under the dining room table or beside you, therefore avoiding the temptation.

OBESITY

Putting a dog on a diet can be quite disheartening for some people. They claim to have cut back on the amount they feed, and their dog still does not lose weight. After speaking with them a short while, it becomes clear why. First, although they may have cut back on the number of crunchies at dinnertime, they still give as many biscuits during the day as they did before. Perhaps they feel sorry for the dog if it begs at the table, so they give it just a taste. Or, perhaps not everyone in the family is sticking to this diet.

I recommend measuring out the amount of food your dog will have during the day for the one or two meals it gets. Put it on the counter, and each time you need to give your dog a treat, take a piece from the bowl instead of a biscuit. The amount of food you have left after breakfast at the end of the day will be the dinner meal, with a few pieces left aside for after-dinner snacks. If you still insist on rewarding your dog with biscuits, buy the smallest ones and only give half of one. Your dog will hardly know the difference. You may also try a cut-up piece of carrot in place of biscuits. My dogs love them! It really should not be a problem for your dog to lose weight. Be firm and remember it is for your dog's good!

TYPES OF FOODS/TREATS

There are three types of commercially available dog food—dry, canned or semimoist—and a huge assortment of treats (lucky dogs!) to feed your dog. Which should you choose?

Dry and canned foods contain similar ingredients. The primary difference between them is their moisture content. The moisture is not just water. It's blood and broth, too, the very things that dogs adore. So while canned food is more palatable, dry food is more economical, convenient and effective in controlling tartar buildup. Most owners feed a 25% canned/75% dry diet to give their dogs the benefit of both. Just be sure your dog is getting the nutrition he needs (you and your veterinarian can determine this).

Semimoist foods have the flavor dogs love and the convenience owners want. However, they tend to contain excessive amounts of artificial colors and preservatives.

Dog treats come in every size, shape and flavor imaginable, from organic cookies shaped like postmen to beefy chew sticks. Dogs seem to love them all, so enjoy the variety. Just be sure not to overindulge your dog. Factor treats into his or her regular meal sizes.

If you try the above and the weight still stays on, consult your veterinarian. There are excellent diet foods available by prescription that work well, and are quite reasonably priced.

WHEN TO FEED

It is advisable to set specific times for your dog to eat rather than free feeding. This will discourage picky eating. Keeping specific time limits for meals may also alert you to a potential problem if your dog stops eating. This is a symptom of many illnesses. Overeating in puppies is a major problem of the free-feeding schedule. A roly-poly puppy may be cute, but it is not healthy.

Grooming

your
Shetland
Sheepdog

One of the decisions you probably made when you were looking at different breeds was how much time you could realistically devote to grooming your dog. The Shetland Sheepdog is a breed that you can easily keep clean and neat, nice to look at and a joy with which to cuddle. There is nothing more beautiful and eye-catching than a Sheltie that has just been groomed, showing himself off!

Grooming requirements for the Shetland Sheepdog are moderate. Of course, your Sheltie must be in good health to have a manageable coat, because poor health encourages a damaged coat. A proper, agreeable diet helps to keep the coat and health in good condition.

The Coat

The double coat can sometimes seem to get away from you, but any amount of thickness can be easily remedied. For those times when you feel you just cannot get the coat under control, by all means phone around and find a reputable professional groomer, and have them start you from scratch. Check with your veterinarian about a well-known and well-respected groomer, one who will have patience with your dog if the coat is a mess. A poor groomer who is not fair to your dog can make the dog forget that grooming can be a pleasant experience, and may undo all your training, and the next time you pick up your brush you may notice your dog is nowhere to be seen!

Routine grooming is best when started early.

You may find that if your dog is a sable, the coat may be coarser and easier to keep, as the blues and tris sometimes have a softer coat that may curl or be wavy.

BRUSHES

Going into a pet store to find a brush can be confusing—there will probably be a full wall of different brushes. Please choose carefully because some brushes will actually break the coat, and make your dog look scraggly.

Each brush is developed to do a different job. Good brushes can be expensive but are worth it, because cheaper ones will not last long and you will have to replace them often. Consult with other Sheltie owners, or a groomer you trust, and find one you think will work for you.

The best brush (and one you can't do without) is a pin brush. Do not get a tiny one—you will need the bigger, heavier one to go through the coat. This will slide easily through the coat with minimum coat breakage. If you do not mind spending a small fortune on a dog brush, the best on the market today is a Mason Pearson bristle brush. It is made from natural bristle and is worth every penny. It will not break the coat and will actually leave a shiny gloss.

You may find you also need to invest in a slicker brush for those times that the coat is thicker and harder to get through. Slicker brushes do tend to pull the hair and break it, so use sparingly and only when needed. A small slicker brush will be easiest to use on the spots that tend to mat quicker—behind the ears and the backs of the hind legs. The area behind the ears is quite sensitive. You must be careful brushing here so you do not irritate the skin. Try to find a soft slicker brush; there are some hard ones on the market, and they can and will damage the skin if used unknowingly with too much force.

Groomed and waiting to get in the showring.

You will also need a comb. I have found the best one is a Greyhound comb. These usually have one end with teeth wider apart, and the other end closer together. Start by using the wider end, and after you are able to slide smoothly through the coat, turn it around and use the other end. This will ensure you are separating each part of the coat. The comb should also be used on the fine, silky hair behind each ear.

If you run a comb through your dog's coat once or twice a week, you will hardly need to de-mat at all! A comb is invaluable when your dog is shedding—it will literally strip out the hair and make your job easier!

BRUSHING

A thorough brushing through the coat once a week will help keep it under control. At an early age there is not the amount of coat to make the job long and tedious. Doing it often with a young pup will get you into the routine, and you will not hate to sit down and look after the coat. Start laying your young puppy down on his side and get him used to being brushed and handled. This will include touching the feet, each toe, lifting up front and back legs, handling and looking into each ear and touching the tail. A lot of Shelties seem to be sensitive about having their tail picked up and brushed.

Benefits from teaching your dog to lie quietly and without resistance include emergency treatment; your dog will not be as stressed lying passively while your veterinarian tends to superficial cuts and wounds. Simple things like tick removal will become less threatening. At this time, you may want to get your dog used to having her temperature taken. You can do this yourself (see Chapter 7 for more information), and if you are nervous about it, ask your veterinarian to show you the procedure.

Be sure to brush your dog's coat when it is slightly damp. This will help prevent breakage of the coat. Buy a squirt bottle and fill it with water. Lightly mist the area you are about to brush. You may even go through a whole bottle of water with each grooming!

The secret to maintaining a healthy, well-brushed coat is to line-brush it. This will get all of the hair shaft, right down to the skin. If you just brush the top of the coat, it will quickly become thick and hard to see or feel the skin. This is not healthy, and is inviting skin problems.

To learn to line-brush, start by lightly brushing the hair on one side. With your dog facing away from you, lying on his side, lightly mist the coat and gently rub in the water. Take your pin brush and brush a line straight up your dog's back (along the backbone), working with a small amount of hair. Start at the roots, and brush upwards so the hair looks like it is spiked down the back. Go back to the start, move down your dog's side a half inch and brush in the same direction, taking another row of hair.

GROOMING TOOLS

pin brush

slicker brush

flea comb

towel

matt rake

grooming glove

scissors

nail clippers

tooth-cleaning equipment

shampoo

conditioner

clippers

You will want to keep a kind of a part going, until you reach your dog's belly. Keep brushing until you've brushed the whole side. Do not forget belly, chest and armpits. Do the feathers on the front and hind legs, too.

After finishing the first side, turn your dog over and repeat on the other side. Be sure to do the neck and front of the chest, too. Reward with a treat right away and you'll be surprised how eager your Sheltie will become when grooming time is near. Do not wait to brush the dog until the coat is thick and matted, and you need to brush and brush and pull on the coat—this definitely is no fun!

If your dog does develop a mat, try to work it free using your fingers. Never bathe a dog with mats—that will make it worse. If the mat will not come apart with your fingers, you can slip one blade of your scissor in and work it out, slicing the hair. You will have some coat loss, but it will help get rid of the mat quicker and easier. Be sure to keep the outside of the scissor against the skin, and the sharp side against the mat, facing away from the dog. Turning the scissors sideways may make you cut the skin. Never pull up on the mat and cut it with scissors—it's really easy to cut the skin this way.

A well-groomed blue merle.

You might try to saturate the mat with straight creme rinse (people brand okay). Work it through and let it soak for a while; it will rinse out during the bath. This may make it easier to comb through after trying to brush through it with your slicker brush.

Bathing

Depending on who you talk to, how often you bathe your dog will vary. My recommendation is to bathe your Sheltie only when dirty. Dirt can and will cut the coat. Never try to bathe your dog without thoroughly brushing him out first. If your dog has a matted coat, bathing before brushing will only tighten the mats, making the eventual brushing out uncomfortable.

Your puppy is ready to learn the bathtub routine at around eight weeks of age. Be very gentle and patient, and do not let him fall or jump out of the tub. For the first few times, do not even shampoo or wet his head. This allows your puppy to gradually get used to bathing and gain confidence.

Always use a shampoo designed for dogs. The dog's pH level is not the same as humans; the average dog has a slightly alkaline skin pH, while human skin has an almost acid pH. Avoid dishwashing detergents and bar soap, which will dry out the coat.

Using your own tub (it is too cold to bathe outside!), place a rubber bath mat in the bottom. This will give your dog better footing, to avoid slipping and becoming scared. Gather everything you will need first, and have it within reach beside the tub. You will need shampoo, cotton balls with which to plug each ear, artificial tears for the eyes, towels (lots of them!), a bucket or cup with which to rinse and something to restrain your dog if necessary. There are some neat restaints available that attach to the wall with a suction cup to hold the dog in the tub. Use only slightly warm water: your dog will not like water that is too hot. Excessively hot water may also dry out the coat unnecessarily.

Start by wetting all the way around the neck, applying shampoo and working it in. Next work down the back and one side, each leg on that side, paying special attention to the hocks, which are usually the dirtiest parts, then turn your dog around and do the same to the other side. Keep your tone happy while bathing:

Shelties are not water dogs! Finish by washing the head. It's a good idea to put one or two cotton balls down deep in the ears—don't worry about touching the eardrum, as it is angled inwards and out of the way. I use a couple of drops of artificial tears (available at any drugstore) in each eye. This will protect the eyes from any irritation from shampoo. Be sure to rinse well—if you are not sure that you have rinsed well enough, rinse again! Leftover shampoo will irritate the skin.

There are many brands of shampoos available, and you may need to try several before you find one with which you are most happy. Whitening shampoos do work, and will make a difference on white areas. There are also shampoos for black coats, sables and even for blues! Talk with your breeder and find out what he or she uses. You can use a human conditioner or a dog one—again, try one and find one you like.

After the bath, towel dry as much as possible. You do not want to let your dog outside until she is absolutely dry. Let your Sheltie shake a few times to get rid of the excess water. Try to pat dry instead of rubbing, which may tangle the coat and make it harder to brush out.

If you bathe your Sheltie outside, make sure you dry her thoroughly.

You may want to use your hair dryer after bathing your dog. This is fine, and a normal occurrence in a grooming shop! Be careful not to let your dog's skin become too hot from the setting. Try a medium setting unless you are able to keep it a good distance from the skin. Try to be able, also, to brush the coat at the same time. This will help it dry much quicker and fluffier. If your dog is worried about the noise, try laying the hairdryer down at a distance to start, leave it running and allowing your dog a chance to get used to the noise.

Trimming the Coat

Trimming your Shetland Sheepdog ranges from easy to difficult, depending on whether your dog is a pet/companion or show dog. Pet owners can easily keep up with the minimal trimming necessary to keep their dogs neat and tidy.

This includes carefully scissoring around the feet, between the pads and a small bit up the back of the front leg, as well as the longer hair some dogs grow on the hock. This will stop some of the dirt, leaves, twigs, etc., from coming in with your dog after a play outside.

Purchase a small, two- or three-inch scissor, which will be much easier for you to use in these areas.

This is about all that's necessary unless you show your dog, and this is where your breeder comes in. Trimming is a fine art that does take some talent and artistic ability. As a rule, the Sheltie should not be a "sculptured" breed, but nowadays you need to learn the intricate details of enhancing your dog's outline, if you want to compete with the top exhibitors.

Trimming the Nails

No grooming collection is complete without nail trimmers. Nail trimmers come in a few different styles. I prefer the guillotine type, because you can purchase replacement blades when they get dull. Another popular style is professional heavy duty, which resembles a big bulky type of scissor, and cuts the nail from both sides, as compared to the guillotine type, which cuts from one side only. Be sure to keep your trimmers sharp, because when they are dull they tend to squish the nail, making the trimming uncomfortable. Start this as soon as you get your puppy; your breeder may have already started getting your dog used to it. This helps ensure less fighting later.

Start out by doing one foot, one nail at a time. Grasp your dog's foot in one hand, trying to hold each toe separately. Make your cut quickly, and without hesitation. Your dog will sense any hesitation and become nervous. Cutting too slowly will only pinch and make it unenjoyable. If you happen to cut a bit close, and you make the quick (the fleshy part inside the nail) bleed, do not worry. It will only sting for a second, and your dog *will not* bleed to death. The worst thing you can do is quit and apologize to him. Just ignore it, add some Quik-Stop (available at any pet store) to stop the bleeding, and continue on. Dogs learn quickly that if they put up a fight, or cry, you will stop and baby them. This does nothing more than make your dog think this behavior is right.

Cut once across the nail, then check underneath it. If you see a tiny black spot or a bit of blood there, that's close enough. If you do not see these, take another cut. If you want to get fancy and do a "professional trim," make a cut off to one side of where you have just cut. Repeat on the other side. These last two cuts will get rid of the sharpness from each side. To get even more fancy, file the sides.

Even youngsters can enjoy grooming!

Reward with a treat even if you are not happy with how your Sheltie behaved. Trimming nails should never be a punishment!

You may wonder how you will know when your dog needs her nails trimmed. If you notice the nails are pointed and have a kind of a hook on the end, it is time. Nails are best kept up if you trim them once a week. Each time you trim them, the quick will recede, and before too long, your dog will be able to sneak up on you across the floor!

Another choice for trimming nails is the electric grinder. You'll have to get your dog used to the noise, and teach her to lie very still on her side. Be careful not to catch the feathering from your dog's legs around the stone. One trick is to place the foot in a stocking and poke the toes through the end. This will help keep the hair away from the grinder. Be very careful—I tried this and caught the grinder on the stocking and pulled the stocking right off my Sheltie's foot!

Do not push on the grinder, just work carefully on each side of the nail. Stop when you notice that tiny black spot mentioned above. It does take longer than simply snipping each nail, but the job it does is fantastic!

Special Hints

A note about what to do if your dog encounters a skunk. Bathe him first in regular shampoo (two baths may be needed). Follow this with the good old tomato juice soak. Pour it on straight, and let him sit with it on for about ten minutes. Rinse it out, and it wouldn't hurt to give him a light spray of doggy cologne (available at any pet store).

Tar and paint are hard to get out of a coated dog. Whatever you do, don't use gasoline, kerosene, turpentine or paint remover. If you must, cut out the bad parts. Try soaking the area instead in vegetable or mineral oil for twenty-four hours, followed by a regular bath.

Gum can be removed with peanut butter. Work it in and bathe to rinse it out. An ice cube rubbed over the gum will "freeze" it, making it easy to break into small pieces and remove from the coat.

chapter 7

Keeping your
Shetland
Sheepdog
Healthy

There is nothing more frustrating than having your dog feel under the weather, and not knowing what you can do to help. If only they could tell us where it hurts. . . . Although they certainly cannot tell us directly, if you pay attention, you will be able to notice certain subtle hints. In a busy family situation, however, it might be easy to miss

warning signs. In order to know when your Sheltie is not healthy, you have to know when your Sheltie is healthy.

Prevention Starts at Day One

Preventive health care will probably be the most important care you can give your dog. First you must start with a healthy, suitable puppy.

This means one that is sound in body and mind. Add to this a correct diet, and the knowledge needed to recognize the signs of good health. This is the best way to help your pal throughout his life. Check with your veterinarian about the availability of pet insurance. There are a few companies that offer pet insurance, which will help you in the time of need for emergencies. Usually, it will not cover routine things like vaccines or spaying or neutering, but it will be there for you when your dog is ill and needs emergency treatments or surgeries. There will be a nominal monthly premium and a deductible, which will be money well spent. It is advised to start purchasing the insurance as soon as you get your new puppy, because some plans will not cover any sickness that has been ongoing.

Most owners will be able to tell when their dog is not feeling well even before their veterinarian can. An owner is attuned to the small details and patterns of his or her dog's daily life. If something changes, it is usually a signal of something wrong. Get into the routine of doing periodic home health checks on your dog. One suggestion is to do so when grooming. This will help you catch health problems before they escalate into something really serious.

To keep your Sheltie happy and healthy, please never try to self-diagnose problems or treat an infection yourself. I realize in this day and age money may be tight, but this could sometimes compromise your dog's life and well-being. It is possible to learn how to recognize some problems and give temporary aid, and you can also learn to treat some common conditions, but I suggest working with your veterinarian and learning some steps you can take to make his or her job easier

FIGHTING FLEAS

Remember, the fleas you see on your dog are only part of the problem—the smallest part! To rid your dog and home of fleas, you need to treat your dog *and* your home. Here's how:

• Identify where your pet(s) sleep. These are "hot spots."

• Clean your pets' bedding regularly by vacuuming and washing.

• Spray "hot spots" with a non-toxic, long-lasting flea larvicide.

• Treat outdoor "hot spots" with insecticide.

• Kill eggs on pets with a product containing insect growth regulators (IGRs).

• Kill fleas on pets per your veterinarian's recommendation.

and perhaps save some time. I will sound like a broken record telling you to call your veterinarian, but, believe me, they would rather hear from you during office hours than in the middle of the night!

A healthy dog looks healthy. He will want to play, be active and will always be ready for his walk. His eyes will be bright, alert and not have any discharge in the corners (except for a small amount in the corners—which is normal).The old adage that a warm nose means the dog is sick is just not true. There should be no discharge from the nostrils, although a small amount of clear dripping is normal. At any signs of mucous, pus or blood, call your veterinarian.

Use tweezers to remove ticks from your dog.

Your dog's ears will be alert and responsive to sounds. There should be no waxy film inside the ear flap, which should be pale pink. It should not smell when you lift it up and look inside. It should not be tender or feel hot to the touch. If the ear does smell pungent or rancid, there is a problem. A sweet smell may be due to a yeast infection. Clean the ears gently with a cotton ball wetted with rubbing alcohol. Sometimes your dog will scratch at her ears, but just like us, dogs have the occasional itch, too! Luckily, Shelties are not prone to ear infections.

Your Sheltie's coat will reflect her good health. It should be shiny, with a minimum of shedding. It should feel nice to touch, not dry or bristly. The skin should be a normal color and free of scabs, sores or bumps. As I mentioned, your dog may itch occasionally, but not excessively. There should be no dandruff. Your Sheltie may have a slight doggy odor, but should not stink. If you house your dog indoors most of the time, you may find the coat will shed all year. This is because the artificial lighting will not regulate

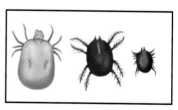

Three types of ticks (l-r): the wood tick, brown dog tick and deer tick.

the coat the way natural light outside will. Your dog may lick excessively at his legs or feet, with the saliva staining the hair a reddish color, and trapping dirt or bacteria. Odor coming from the feet area could be infected sweat glands in the feet.

Another source of odor could be flatulence. This is usually traced to diet, which may be high in proteins like beans or soybean meal. Switch your dog to a easily digested low-fiber diet. Greedy eaters routinely swallow a lot of air while eating, thus causing gas.

GOOD NUTRITION

Proper nutrition will play a large part in keeping your dog healthy. Remember the old saying "You are what you eat"? Well, it's true. Your dog will look and feel better given a complete and balanced diet, which will, in turn, ensure he lives a full and lengthy life and keep your visits to the veterinarian to a minimum.

DENTAL HEALTH

Check your dog's teeth frequently and brush them regularly.

Lift up the lips and you should see healthy, clean white teeth and gums. Normal gums will be slightly moist, dry gums could be a signal of dehydration. Dental plaque accumulates, worst on the very back teeth (molars), and this will cause inflammation to the gums. This could lead to gum recession and teeth loss. This is the most common cause of foul smell around your dog, sometimes being missed as the source of the odor. Food particles get caught in the teeth, and a persistent smell may be signaling periodontal disease. This is often due to accumulation of soft bacterial plaque and hard tartar on and between teeth or, in extreme cases, under the gum. Bacteria flourishes in the warm, moist environment of the mouth, releasing sulfur-containing compounds that smell. If there's odor, have your dog's mouth examined. Following a dental checkup, you will be surprised how good your dog feels!

You can easily get your dog used to having you brush her teeth, preventing a lot of discomfort to the dog and large veterinarian bills for you. Start by slipping a finger or two into your dog's mouth. Rub over the teeth, and call it quits for the day. Reward with a biscuit. Each day, take longer to do this. After about a week, you will be able to put some doggy toothpaste on a baby toothbrush, and brush your dog's teeth. Do not use people toothpaste, as it is meant to be spit out. As our friends cannot spit, be sure to buy a paste labeled for dogs. This is easy to find at your pet store or from your veterinarian. If you get into the routine of doing this once a day, or even once a week, it will dramatically cut down the number of dentals your dog will need from your veterinarian.

Dental care can be helped along with a couple of good products. First of all, I suggest beginning these following a dental scaling and polishing done by your veterinarian. This is when the teeth are shiny clean and you can start from scratch. I've previously mentioned the importance of dry food. This will cause a scraping action, continually removing plaque. Plaque is unfortunately there again once the dog stops chewing. Where we're concerned is below the gumline, where bacteria and plaque hide, rotting the teeth and bone. Most things will only help above the gumline.

A healthy Sheltie enjoys a game of Frisbee.

Bacterial infection from badly infected and dirty teeth can invade your dog's blood stream. It can be associated with heart problems and other organ disorders. Odor can also be present if your dog has a broken tooth, exposing pulp tissue, which then dies and causes infection to develop within a root canal. This is very smelly, and involves extraction or root canals. Mouth tumors; diseases of the pharynx, nasal cavity, sinuses, esophagus; liver dysfunction; bowel disease and pancreatic disorders can all cause bad breath.

Dogs with kidney disease will also have bad breath, due to a high blood urea level. This may not be evident until too late; by then the dog may be vomiting and the disease may be quite advanced. It is vital that your veterinarian screen your dog's blood for kidney disease before any anesthesia is ever given.

Bad breath is also common for those dogs that eat feces. The correct term for this bad habit (they do not lack anything in their diet!) is coprophagia. Picking up stools promptly will help break your dog of this habit. A product quite successful in stopping this is called Forbid. Used three days in a row, it will dissuade your dog from this disgusting habit.

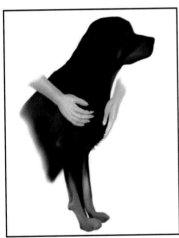

Run your hands regularly over your dog to feel for any injuries.

ANAL GLANDS

Anal glands may sometimes cause your dog much discomfort. Some dogs are bothered a lot, and some go through life never needing to have them checked. The anal glands are on either side of the rectum, and may need occasional expressing. They are normally expressed by your dog during a bowel movement. At times, they may be explosively expressed by your dog in stressful or frightening situations. They are often referred to as the scent glands, because it is believed that this is how dogs mark their territory. If not emptied by a bowel movement, they may become plugged, so if you notice your dog scooting his rear, or chewing at his hind end, this could be the problem. The glands contain a liquid brownish secretion, which has a foul smell. If they become impacted and full, and not checked by your veterinarian, the anal glands could rupture, requiring a trip to the veterinarian anyway. Antibiotics are needed, and in some cases your dog may need to have anesthesia in order for your veterinarian to unplug them.

If your dog is continually bothered by his anal glands, talk to your veterinarian about having them removed. Expressing them yourself is something you can learn to do at home—the best time to do this is at bath time. This way the smell and mess can be washed away. Ask your veterinarian for a lesson the next time you take your dog in.

TAKING A TEMPERATURE

The first thing you can do if you notice your dog is not her usual self is to take her temperature. Purchase a rectal thermometer and keep it handy with your basic first aid kit. Shake it down each time before using. Lubricate it with petroleum jelly, and gently insert it into the rectum. It does not need to go in all the way, about halfway is good. Leave it there for at least one minute, then withdraw gently, wipe with a tissue and take the reading. The normal temperature for a dog is 101.5 degrees Fahrenheit, and a variance of five degrees or so is not cause for alarm. Take note of your dog's temperature, as this can be a valuable reference.

TAKING A PULSE

To check your dog's pulse, you can have your dog standing or lying down. Place your hand around your dog's hind leg, with your index finger inside the hind leg as high up as you can reach, or about mid thigh. You should find the pulse easily. The normal heart/pulse rate is 70 to 120 beats per minute.

ADMINISTERING MEDICATION

Administering medications can be simple if your dog is used to being handled.

Pills and liquid medications: To give your dog liquid medications, use a syringe without the needle. In a hurry, a turkey baster can also do the job. Most liquids can be slowly syringed into the side of the mouth. With one hand, steady the head by grasping the muzzle over the top, tipping the head back. With the syringe in your other hand, slowly lift up the lips with the fingers that are steadying the head and forming a pocket, then squeeze the plunger, as far back in the mouth as you can, until all the liquid is out. Gently stroke the lower jaw to encourage swallowing. I usually follow with a treat of some kind. Remember, this should not be a worry for your dog.

YOUR PUPPY'S VACCINES

Vaccines are given to prevent your dog from getting an infectious disease like canine distemper or rabies. Vaccines are the ultimate preventive medicine: they're given before your dog ever gets the disease so as to protect him from the disease. That's why it is necessary for your dog to be vaccinated routinely. Puppy vaccines start at eight weeks of age for the five-in-one DHLPP vaccine and are given every three to four weeks until the puppy is sixteen months old. Your veterinarian will put your puppy on a proper schedule and will remind you when to bring in your dog for shots.

To give pills, open the mouth with your thumb on one side and index finger on the other, over the top jaw. With your other hand, pull down on the lower jaw with your little finger. I hold the pill in with my thumb and index finger. Push the pill back as far as you can and as quickly as possible. Don't delay, as your dog may be fighting against you. Gently hold the mouth closed and wait until your dog swallows. Many dogs are experts at bluffing you, making you think they have swallowed the pill, and you later find it under the couch!

I caution against simply putting the liquid or tablet medication in your dog's food, because if your dog does not eat all his food, the medication will not be completely effective.

Eye and ear medication: You may be nervous about applying eye ointments or drops. Don't worry! Once you catch on, it's really quite simple. To apply ointment, usually all that is needed is a thin line easily squeezed inside the lower lid. Pull down on the lower lid, and put a thin line of ointment along the lid. Close the eyelid when you are done, to help move the ointment over the eyeball. Slip your dog a treat and she will actually begin to look forward to treatment time!

Eye drops are done similarly. Tip your dog's head back, pull down on the lower lid and drop it in. Try to hold the bottle as close to the eye as possible to prevent the drop from missing the eye.

Ear drops need to be applied as deep into the ear as possible. You will want to hold the ear in one hand, and stick the dropper as deep down as you can. After dispensing the required amount, massage the ear at the base to help distribute the medication. You will know you are doing it right if you hear a squishy sound. Always be sure to put the lids back on tightly.

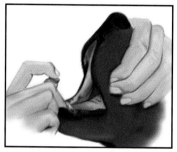

To give a pill, open the mouth wide, then drop it in the back of the throat.

With any medications, please follow your doctor's instructions all the way until it is finished. Even if you feel your dog has made a full recovery, finish the medication. If you stop halfway through, your dog may not have received enough medication and the ailment may return at a later date. The same prescription may not work as well a second time if it was not finished on the first go. Also, please discard any medication after it has expired. Don't fool around with outdated antibiotics or eye drops or anything. They have expiration dates for a reason.

Squeeze eye ointment into the lower lid.

Diseases and Viruses
DISTEMPER

Distemper is not common in dogs today. Extremely effective vaccines have made this disease almost invisible. It still surfaces in some areas in epidemic proportions, however, so it should not be dismissed entirely.

73

It is a highly infectious, frequently fatal viral disease that usually affects puppies under one year of age. The virus itself is very fragile and is rapidly destroyed outside the body, so direct contact is the only method of infection.

Symptoms will be a cough, and your dog will begin to have a mild discharge from his eyes and nose. This will become quite thick. The eyes will become very inflamed and red, and the discharge from the nose will dry in the nostrils, making it difficult for your dog to breathe.

Shortly after this, the lining of the stomach and intestine will be affected, resulting in vomiting and diarrhea which will sometimes contain blood. Your dog will feel miserable, have a temperature of up to 104 degrees, not eat his food and want to sleep all the time. These symptoms last about three weeks. Next, the disease will attack the skin. The pads of the feet will become thickened and hard.

Prevention keeps your Sheltie in peak form.

After surviving the first stages, some dogs may begin to show nervous symptoms, usually around four weeks or so. The virus will be attacking the brain at this point, causing fits, twitching or jerking and paralysis. Untreated cases will develop pneumonia, possibly causing your dog to die. Because it is a viral infection, there is no specific cure for distemper. Your veterinarian will try to control the secondary bacterial infections by prescribing antibiotics.

Acute infections will respond easily to cough medicines or antibiotics. Rest is essential, and exercise should be restricted until the dog is better. Some respiratory infections are highly contagious, and affected dogs should be kept isolated until the cough has gone.

"Kennel Cough"

"Kennel cough" is one of the first diseases thought of when a dog is coughing. It is a respiratory infection usually occurring in dogs that are kenneled together. Even a single dog can easily pick it up meeting another infected dog while out for a walk. A few different infections actually cause "kennel cough."

One of these is *Bordetella bronchiseptica*. It causes an upper respiratory tract infection with a cough and nasal discharge. This bacterium is also an important secondary invader following viral respiratory infection. Young dogs are more often affected than older dogs. The incubation period for "kennel cough" varies from two to ten days.

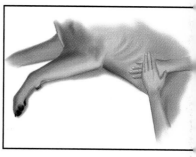

The cough is moist and hacking, and sometimes your dog will bring up a foamy froth. Retching and gagging are frequent. Bouts of coughing are spontaneous but can be brought on by excitement. There can be a nasal discharge. Depression, loss of appetite, fever and tonsillitis may occur.

Applying abdominal thrusts can save a choking dog.

Treatment is started with antibiotics, because *Bordetella* bacteria are frequently involved as a primary or secondary infection. Some cases will easily clear up in days, and others could drag on for months. Your dog should be kept warm and dry. Softening the food will help it go down easier. Some cough medicines help. In old or debilitated dogs, pneumonia may follow, and sometimes death. "Kennel cough" caused by *Bordetella* can be controlled easily with routine vaccinations given right into your dog's nostrils. Try to make it one of your dog's routine vaccinations. Prevention costs less and is much easier on your dog!

75

Another virus that may cause "kennel cough" is *parain-fluenza.* Infections are common, but signs are mild unless it accompanies *Bordetella.* Time of infection will be about one to nine days after coming in contact with another infected dog. Incubation will take about two to eight days.

Fever is an early sign, but it is typically only one half to one degree above normal. A dry, nonproductive cough lasts for several days, but seldom more than a week. Sneezing and mild eye and nose discharges are common. Tonsillitis may appear. Antibiotics are used to control secondary bacterial infections. Routine vaccinations will include this disease.

Canine adenovirus can also contribute to "kennel cough." Signs are a dry cough, nose and eye discharge and swollen tonsils. In severe cases, dyspnea is apparent. Fever, dullness and depressed appetite may be present, but no other signs are usually seen.

HEPATITIS

Hepatitis is a disease of the liver. It can occur in mild or severe forms. Usually young, unvaccinated dogs are affected. The incubation period for hepatitis is about two weeks.

Symptoms are a slight loss of appetite, listlessness, and a raised temperature. Recovery may be quick, and sometimes the disease is not diagnosed until recovery. A bluish look to the eye will be a key factor in diagnosing this disease. It should clear within two weeks.

In severe cases, your dog will not eat at all, be very dull and depressed and may collapse. Some die suddenly, with no warning that anything is wrong. The temperature will be over 104 degrees to start and your dog will show signs of discomfort in the abdomen, due to a painful, swollen liver, making him restless. Vomiting might occur and may contain blood. Gums and lips will seem pale, with small dots of bleeding in them for a few days. Jaundice may occur, but is atypical. Dogs suffering this severe form are unlikely to recover.

Treatment given is for symptoms only. Drugs may be needed to stop vomiting. Antibiotics are of no use, as this disease spreads so rapidly there is no secondary bacterial infection.

The virus is spread by urine, feces and saliva, and recovered dogs can continue to spread it for six months afterward. Hepatitis is a very stable virus and can exist for ten days outside the body and environment.

LEPTOSPIROSIS

Leptospirosis consists of two separate forms of the organism. One causes acute kidney disease, the other causes acute infection in the liver, often leading to jaundice. Both forms are infectious to humans.

This disease is usually transmitted through infected urine that may be licked or inhaled by a dog out for a walk. The organisms invade the bloodstream for a week or so before attacking the kidney tissue. During this time, your dog may have no symptoms. After the incubation period, the signs become more severe, with depression, total disinterest in food, excessive thirst and urination, vomiting and abdominal pain over the kidneys. Mouth ulcers and an unpleasant smell to the breath may develop if the kidneys become severely infected. This may lead to death, or your veterinarian may suggest euthanasia because of the low chance of recovery. Leptospirosis can be treated with some antibiotics, and in severe cases intravenous fluids

---

A FIRST-AID KIT

Keep a canine first-aid kit on hand for general care and emergencies. Check it periodically to make sure liquids haven't spilled or dried up, and replace medications and materials after they're used. Your kit should include:

Activated charcoal tablets

Adhesive tape
(1 and 2 inches wide)

Antibacterial ointment
(for skin and eyes)

Aspirin (buffered or enteric coated, *not* Ibuprofen)

Bandages: Gauze rolls (1 and 2 inches wide) and dressing pads

Cotton balls

Diarrhea medicine

Dosing syringe

Hydrogen peroxide (3%)

Petroleum jelly

Rectal thermometer

Rubber gloves

Rubbing alcohol

Scissors

Tourniquet

Towel

Tweezers

---

may be given. If your dog recovers, he may be left with damaged kidneys, which is thought to lead to chronic kidney disease in the older dog.

The second form of this disease affects the liver, and is also very serious. It is mainly a country disease, and rats frequently act as carriers to both man and dog. It is also transmitted through their urine.

The virus will enter the body through the mouth or nose. After entering the bloodstream, it attacks the liver. Onset of illness is very sudden, and very severe. Your dog becomes dull and depressed, due to a high temperature. The eyes, gums and skin become yellow, because of jaundice. Vomiting and diarrhea occur, and the dog will be thirsty. Your dog will go downhill rapidly, and death can occur within a few hours of the first symptoms.

Antibiotics may stop the massive infection of the liver and stop the disease from spreading if caught early enough, although once the liver is affected to the extent of jaundice, treatment is usually ineffective. Because of the risk of infection to humans, euthanasia is usually recommended.

> ## WHEN TO CALL THE VET
>
> In any emergency situation, you should call your veterinarian immediately. You can make the difference in your dog's life by staying as calm as possible when you call and by giving the doctor or the assistant as much information as possible before you leave for the clinic. That way, the vet will be able to take immediate, specific action to remedy your dog's situation.
>
> Emergencies include acute abdominal pain, suspected poisoning, snakebite, burns, frostbite, shock, dehydration, abnormal vomiting or bleeding, and deep wounds. You are the best judge of your dog's health, as you live with and observe him every day. Don't hesitate to call your veterinarian if you suspect trouble.

PARVOVIRUS

Until 1978, no one had heard of parvovirus. The virus is very resistant to environmental changes and can live outside the body for well over a year.

Infection occurs when your dog takes the virus into her mouth. This commonly occurs through direct contact with affected dogs or their feces. Your dog can also become infected by sniffing an area where feces have been for months. You can even bring the virus home yourself on your shoes or clothing. Most common in puppies, dogs of any age may be susceptible. The death rate in the twelve-week age group is about 10 percent. Signs usually are sudden, with vomiting, depression, loss of appetite and bloody diarrhea. It may be hard to stop the vomiting, and your dog can become dehydrated in no time. Death from dehydration may occur as rapidly as two or three days without treatment.

RABIES

Rabies. The name alone puts fear into everyone's mind. It is an all too real disease that is very transmissible to humans. Your dog can become infected from the bite of a wild animal—raccoons, skunks, foxes, etc. A more common transmitter is the bat. The virus is spread by the saliva, which enters the body from a bite wound.

The average incubation period is two to three weeks, but nine months is not unusual. Depending on where the bite is on the dog, the incubation time and arrival of symptoms will vary. If the wound is near the head, the disease will spread quickly. The virus travels to the brain along nerve networks, beginning with the spinal cord, then slowly to the brain. At this point, your dog will not show any symptoms, and the original wound will have healed. Once the virus hits the brain, it will move to the salivary glands and into the mouth. This is when it can be spread to another animal through a bite.

The most noticeable symptom is a personality change. A typically affectionate Sheltie might turn irritable or aggressive. A shy or less-outgoing one may turn affectionate. Your dog may withdraw and stare out into space. He will avoid light because his eyes will be sore due to "photophobia." At the end, the dog will not want to be touched or handled. Fever, vomiting and diarrhea are common.

Many people tell stories about a dog foaming at the mouth. This is characteristic of the paralytic form of the disease because the muscles of the head become paralyzed. Your dog will not be able swallow or close her mouth and the tongue may hang out. The furious form of rabies is the "mad dog" type. Your dog will become suspicious or aggressive, attacking anything that moves. The muscles in the face spasm, causing the lips to be drawn back and exposing the teeth.

Dogs that spend a lot of time outdoors are most susceptible to Lyme disease

In both forms, death usually follows within five days.

You should not handle a dog you suspect has rabies. The dog needs to be impounded. There is no effective treatment for dogs. To protect yourself and your dog, please keep rabies vaccinations current!

LYME DISEASE

Lyme disease is spreading quite rapidly across the country. Spread by ticks, this disease affects dogs and humans. First reported in 1975, it is now the most frequently reported tick-borne disease transmitted to people. Lyme disease causes fever, loss of appetite, arthritis, sudden pain and lameness, lethargy and depression. If left untreated, the disease advances to signs of chronic arthritis, heart-muscle damage, brain and spinal cord invasion and even kidney failure.

Swollen joints and lameness, local inflammation around the bite, and reluctance to play will be the first signs that something is wrong with your dog. This may be followed by more generalized infection throughout the body to all parts. This ends with the final retreat of the organism from the immune system, generally hiding in the joints or nervous system. Death due to kidney failure is possible. This is why research of this disease is being pursued quite avidly.

Luckily, most dogs bought from reputable breeders come from parents that have been vaccinated, providing them with necessary protection, and the puppies are always started on vaccinations before going into a new home.

DIARRHEA

Even the healthiest dogs may experience an occasional bout of diarrhea. It can be brought on by a sudden change in diet, table scraps, water changes or stress. Never take this lightly, as it can certainly be telling you there is a problem. A call to the veterinarian would be a good idea, and he or she may suggest a diet of boiled rice and lean hamburger for the next twenty-four to forty-eight hours. Restrict water intake a little, offering ice cubes to lick instead. Refrain from feeding the normal diet for at least one to two days. Gradually reintroduce your dog back to her normal diet over a couple of days. Try to think of the reason this has happened, and stay away from the possible cause. If any blood shows up in the stool, definitely contact your veterinarian.

Some of the many household substances harmful to your dog.

VOMITING

Vomiting can also be caused by dietary upsets. Your dog may repeatedly vomit either food or stomach fluid, which may end up bloodstained. Withhold food and water (except ice cubes) for twenty-four hours, and contact your veterinarian. Depending on the diagnosis, your veterinarian may prescribe antibiotics or gastric sedatives.

Internal Parasites

A good program of routine worming will help you avoid problems. You should do so at least once a year (a good time to pick up wormer is when you are at your veterinarian's for yearly vaccinations). If you want to be

These specks in your dog's fur mean he has fleas.

extremely vigilant against worms, deworm your dog every six months. I recommend purchasing your dog's wormer from your veterinarian because pet stores may not have the most up-to-date types and may misinform you of the type of worm your dog has based on your description. If in doubt, collect a sample of the worm, pop it into a pill vial and take it to your veterinarian for identification.

ROUNDWORMS

The most common type of worm in a young puppy is the round-worm. Puppies are usually wormed for the first time as young as two to three weeks of age, and are given repeat treatments usually ten days apart—the time it takes to kill eggs that were in the larvae stage at the first deworming. Deworming the dam before or during pregnancy does not prevent infestations of puppies, because medications don't work on larvae that are already encysted.

Puppies can infect themselves through contact with dirt containing eggs or from the dam. In a breeding

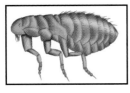

female, during the latter stages of pregnancy, dormant larvae are released, reenter the circulation and are carried to the unborn puppies. They can also be passed on to the puppies through nursing. Adult dogs do not usually have much problem with roundworms.

The flea is a die-hard pest.

Puppies may have a potbellied appearance if they have a heavy infestation. They may have a dull coat. Usually, signs are vomiting, sometimes bringing up worms; diarrhea; weight loss and an overall unthrifty look. Young puppies can dehydrate very quickly and can die within two to three weeks of birth. You may notice worms passed in the stool, and they will resemble spaghetti.

TAPEWORM

The second most common type of worm is the tapeworm. These look like a dried piece of rice, usually found in the hair around the dog's rectum. Segments can also be passed in the stool. These are acquired by a dog through fleas—the intermediate host. Flea control must be stepped up when you come across tapeworms. Dogs will unintentionally eat fleas while chewing at themselves to scratch flea bites. The segments around the rectum may become itchy, causing the dog to scoot along the floor. This is sometimes confused with anal gland irritation.

There is another type of tapeworm that is acquired by a dog if he eats raw, wild meat. For this reason, dogs should never be fed raw organ meat from sheep or wild animals. This is not as common as the flea tapeworm.

HOOKWORMS

Exercise is important for your dog's health.

If overlooked, hookworms can seriously weaken or kill a dog. These bloodsucking parasites can cause anemia in puppies and adults. Signs of hookworm infection include weakness, pale gums, weight loss and dehydration. The stool can be dark and tarry or your dog may have diarrhea containing mucus and blood. This resembles parvovirus, so your veterinarian should be contacted to rule this out. Hookworms commonly are passed to puppies through their mother's milk. They can also enter your dog's system by penetrating the skin of the feet or body. They will burrow into the tissues and migrate to the lungs. Dogs may develop an itchy rash where the larvae enter the skin. Hookworms can also be picked up by ingesting a secondary or intermediate host, carrying the worm inside itself until eaten by the dog. Small rodents, crickets, beetles and cockroaches can carry the larvae.

WHIPWORMS

Diarrhea, sometimes containing blood, is a symptom of whipworm. The loss of blood can cause anemia, making your dog more susceptible to disease. Routine wormers usually do not include medication for this type of worm. Confirm infestation with a stool sample, and follow with a specific wormer to rid your dog of this problem. Whipworm eggs can survive in the environment for several years. Several months of sunshine and dry weather are required before the area is safe for pets again.

HEARTWORM

Heartworm infection is transmitted by the bite of a mosquito. Adult worms live in the heart and lungs of a dog and their offspring (microfilaria) circulate in the bloodstream. Even if your dog does not go outside or come in contact with other dogs, she can still be at risk. The prevalence of this disease will vary depending on the area in which you live. It is most common in places that are warm and moist all year round (which is where mosquitos thrive). Check with your veterinarian about the risk in your area.

The adult heartworm can cause severe illness and even death due to congestive heart failure and/or emboli (blood clots) in the lungs. Clinical signs are liver problems, coughing and weight loss. X rays can confirm your veterinarian's suspicions.

IDENTIFYING YOUR DOG

It's a terrible thing to think about, but your dog could somehow, someday, get lost or stolen. How would you get him back? Your best bet would be to have some form of identification on your dog. You can choose from a collar and tags, a tattoo, a microchip or a combination of these three.

Every dog should wear a buckle collar with identification tags. They are the quickest and easiest way for a stranger to identify your dog. It's best to inscribe the tags with your name and phone number; you don't need to include your dog's name.

There are two ways to permanently identify your dog. The first is a tattoo, placed on the inside of your dog's thigh. The tattoo should be your social security number or your dog's AKC registration number.

The second is a microchip, a rice-sized pellet that's inserted under the dog's skin at the base of the neck, between the shoulder blades. When a scanner is passed over the dog, it will beep, notifying the person that the dog has a chip. The scanner will then show a code, identifying the dog. Microchips are becoming more and more popular and are certainly the wave of the future.

There are two tests to find out if your dog has heartworm. The first is a filter test, which checks a blood sample for microfilaria. The other looks for antigens (foreign bodies) shed by the heartworm. This test can pick up cases the filter test missed if the heartworm were not reproducing.

Heartworm is easily prevented if you know how, but please seek the advice of your veterinarian. If your dog tests positive to heartworm, the treatment may include hospitalization. Treatment is more successful if your dog is still in good physical shape. Arsenic, needing careful dosing, is used to kill the adult worms, and a second drug later is used to kill the microfilaria. Although the arsenic kills the adults, the dead worms are still in the heart and lungs, and must be slowly broken down by the body's defenses. Serious emboli (blood clots) can occur during this time.

Common internal parasites (l-r): roundworm, whipworm, tapeworm and hookworm.

COCCIDIA

Coccidia infests the intestines of dogs, but is different from the worms described above. This parasite lives in the cells lining the intestines. Young dogs can become seriously affected, getting the parasite from older dogs, which may not show any signs. Diarrhea shows upon the third day after infection, blood can appear after the sixth day. Dehydration and anemia, with weight loss and weakness, will appear in severe cases. If your dog survives, the diarrhea will seem to contain gelatin as the intestines start to heal. A dog confined to a yard can reinfect itself.

GIARDIA

Giardia is another parasite spread by contaminated drinking water. It is similar to *Coccidiosis* in that it affects the cells lining the intestines. Diarrhea and bloody stools are the usual signs, and a fecal sample is needed to confirm the eggs or cysts in the stool. Dogs respond quite well to treatment.

Special Considerations
SPAYING AND NEUTERING

Altering your dog is a simple operation done at an early age—usually six to nine months. It requires a day stay at the veterinarian's, and most dogs act like nothing was even done. The cost is extremely reasonable—it lasts a lifetime! If you are unsure what to expect the day of surgery, maybe this will help you to understand the procedure.

You will be asked to fast your dog (no food or water) from suppertime the evening before. This is to be sure your dog's stomach is empty, for the same reasons we humans must also fast before anesthesia.

Your dog will be admitted in the morning, given a preanesthetic injection and placed in a kennel for ten to fifteen minutes while the injection takes effect. Your veterinarian will then inject the anesthesia into your dog's forearm. This will take effect immediately.

The dog is then intubated with a trachea tube to ensure a clear airway for the oxygen/anesthetic and then hooked up to the inhalant gas. Your dog will be placed on her back and the belly area is shaved and washed. Your veterinarian makes an incision, which may require anywhere from two to three sutures to close. These sutures are removed anywhere from ten to twelve days after the surgery.

ADVANTAGES OF SPAY/NEUTER

The greatest advantage of spaying (for females) or neutering (for males) your dog is that you are guaranteed your dog will not produce puppies. There are too many puppies already available for too few homes. There are other advantages as well.

ADVANTAGES OF SPAYING

No messy heats.

No "suitors" howling at your windows or waiting in your yard.

Decreased incidences of pyometra (disease of the uterus) and breast cancer.

ADVANTAGES OF NEUTERING

Lessens male aggressive and territorial behaviors, but doesn't affect the dog's personality. Behaviors are often owner-induced, so neutering is not the only answer, but it is a good start.

Prevents the need to roam in search of bitches in season.

Decreased incidences of urogenital diseases.

The female's surgery takes an average of fifteen to twenty minutes total. The uterus and ovaries are removed, which will prevent her from coming into season.

I hear many people say that they want their female dog to have a litter so their kids can see the "miracle of birth." I reply by saying that they should take their kids to the local humane society to witness the high number of dogs being euthanized because of a lack of homes, therefore also witnessing the "miracle of death." Why add to this growing statistic? If you are going to breed your dog, do it for the right reason. Waiting until your dog is older before spaying or neutering can cause problems with both the male and female. Be safe and spay or neuter your dog at an early age.

Male dog's surgery includes removal of the testicles. Vasectomies are not routinely performed, as your dog may still exhibit the very traits for which most dogs are neutered: fighting and marking territory, etc. His surgery takes less time than the female's surgery and his stay will be brief, usually ready to be picked up at the end of the day.

THE MALE DOG

If your male dog is not neutered, keep an eye on his testicles. Any change in shape or size could signal a potential problem. Infection or orchitis is very rare, but when it shows up, one or both testicles become very painful and swollen. The dog will have a raised temperature, lack of appetite and reluctance to move. This responds quickly to antibiotics, but an abscess may occur. In some cases, surgical removal may be necessary.

Tumors are fairly common, but luckily most are benign. If allowed to become large, it may interfere with walking. The "Sertoli cell" tumor produces female hormones, causing your dog to develop female characteristics. The mammary glands and teats enlarge, and he will become attractive to other male dogs. Hair loss may begin in equal amounts on each flank. In this case again, neutering is recommended treatment and the changes will invariably reverse.

Torsion, where the testicle twists around its base and stops the blood supply, occurs very rarely but is common in retained testicle(s). Very painful, your dog will have a very tense abdomen, will vomit and be reluctant to move. Blood supply loss will cause tissue damage. Treatment is emergency surgical removal.

Intact dogs can also be troubled by prostate infections. You may notice your dog dripping bloody urine. He may be subdued, not interested in his food, have a raised temperature and pain in the abdomen or be reluctant to move. He may also strain to urinate and may appear constipated.

Immediate veterinarian attention is needed. This infection can be hard to clear up, and may be stubborn with antibiotics. Upon a rectal palpation, your veterinarian will be able to detect a large and painful prostate gland. It is painful for your dog, and treatment is usually started with having the dog neutered. (Another reason to have this done at an early age!)

If you are not going to show or breed your Sheltie, please have him neutered and her spayed. Show rules and regulations state that a dog or bitch cannot be neutered or spayed if they are to be shown. This is supposedly to prove that the dog or bitch is capable of reproducing his or her own quality.

THE AGING SHELTIE

As your dog ages, certain things may crop up that require attention—from dental problems to growths that must always be investigated, if not removed and biopsied.

Older pets should be checked by your veterinarian at least once, preferably twice, a year. And don't forget to keep up with vaccinations! The office call for vaccinations usually includes the examination, so take advantage of it. Your veterinarian will listen to your dog's heart, possibly picking up on a heart murmur that's begun, or check for a defective valve, or heartworms. The examination will also include a full check of the lungs for congestion or fluid; the mouth for dental problems or abnormalities; the tonsils for inflammation; the ears; the eyes for redness, change or cloudiness of the eyeball; the lymph nodes under the chin and front of the shoulder blades; the neck area for pinched nerves or cervical disc problems; the abdomen for any masses, usually being able to feel the liver, spleen, small and large intestine, kidneys and bladder. Your veterinarian will also examine your dog's skin for any lumps, bumps, swollen areas or evidence of fleas or ticks and will check your dog's temperature.

Some skin afflictions may seem innocuous to you, but your veterinarian's trained eye may be able to catch a potential problem early.

"Hot spots" may be something you run into during your Sheltie's life. If your dog scratches or chews at itself, it could cause damage. The more your dog digs and chews, the worse it will get. If left untreated, the condition can spread and become a secondary infection. Within twenty-four hours, the spot can grow into a two- or three-inch area that will be raw with possible blood and greenish slime on it. These are actually like burns, hence the name "hot spot." The skin will be extremely painful, and permanent hair loss may result.

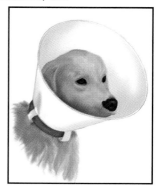

To combat the problem, you should trim as much hair as possible from the area, wash it with Hibitane skin cleanser (available at a pharmacy), and prevent your dog from getting at it. An Elizabethan collar may be necessary to stop additional damage. Do not try to cover the area with a bandage: it needs to be open to heal. Your veterinarian may prescribe antibiotics, antihistamines or sedatives to promote healing. Once your dog stops bugging the area,

An Elizabethan collar keeps your dog from licking a fresh wound.

89

it will quickly begin to heal within a few days. Hot spots are not contagious to people or other pets.

As your dog ages, she will start to slow down, have trouble getting up, sleep longer, lose a bit of hearing, develop a "glazed over" look in the eyes, and will be less apt to jump up on your bed.

The most common life-threatening problems with older dogs are cancer, kidney, liver and heart disease. If caught early enough, with proper care and treatment, many dogs can live several more years.

First Aid

First Aid should never be used as a substitute for professional care, but it can help save your Sheltie's life.

Make a temporary splint by wrapping the leg in firm casing, then bandaging it.

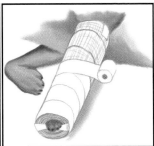

BLEEDING

Bleeding from a severe cut or wound must be stopped right away. There are two basic techniques—direct pressure and the tourniquet.

Try to control bleeding first by using direct pressure. Ask a friend to hold your injured Sheltie and place several pads of sterile gauze over the wound. Press. Do not wipe the wound or apply any cleansers or ointments. Apply firm, even pressure. If blood soaks through the pad, do not remove it as this could disrupt clotting. Simply place another pad on top and continue to apply pressure.

If bleeding on a leg or the tail does not stop by applying pressure, try using a tourniquet. Use this only as a last resort. A tourniquet that is left on too long can result in limb loss. To apply a tourniquet, do the following:

1. Wrap the limb or tail with one-inch gauze or a wide piece of cloth slightly above the wound and tie a half knot. Do not use a narrow band, rope or wire.

2. Place a pencil or stick on top and finish the knot.

3. Twist the pencil slowly until the bleeding stops. Fasten in place with tape.

4. Cover the wound with sterile gauze.

5. Once the tourniquet is on, take your dog to your veterinarian right away.

If your Sheltie is bleeding from her mouth or anus, or vomits or defecates blood, she may be suffering from internal injuries. Do not attempt to stop bleeding. Call your veterinarian right away for emergency treatment.

SHOCK

Trauma, such as being hit by a car, blood loss, burns or allergic reactions, can cause a condition known as shock. Shock is a collapse of the circulatory system. It occurs when the volume of circulating blood is decreased or the blood vessels collapse, and the heart loses its ability to pump blood. The decreased supply of oxygen to the tissues usually results in unconsciousness, pale gums, weak, rapid pulse and labored, rapid breathing.

Shock can be difficult to recognize, but it must be treated right away because it can be fatal. If your dog is in shock:

1. Stop bleeding or give CPR as necessary.

2. Allow your dog to adopt a position in which she is most comfortable.

3. Cover with a towel or blanket.

4. If your dog is unconscious, clear her airways and slightly elevate her rear end. This will assist in blood flow to the brain.

5. Do not give your dog water. Due to decreased blood circulation, the digestive tract cannot absorb the water efficiently.

6. Do not muzzle your dog. This may impair breathing.

7. Transport your dog to the veterinary clinic on a stretcher, flat board or hammock for treatment right away.

CPR

Cardiopulmonary resuscitation, commonly called CPR, is a life-saving technique that provides artificial breathing and heart contractions for an unconscious animal whose heart and breathing have stopped. CPR combines artificial breathing with heart massage. Artificial respiration alone can be used for animals suffering respiratory distress—when not combined with cardiac arrest—to aid breathing.

Dogs can suffer respiratory and cardiac failure for many reasons, including being hit by a car, poisoning or electrical shock. Respiratory distress is caused by many conditions, including a foreign object in the nasal passages, chest wounds or tearing of the diaphragm.

Do not attempt to perform CPR on a dog who has a heartbeat, or perform artificial respiration on a conscious dog, unless his breathing is extremely shallow. In these instances, the life-saving techniques can harm your dog.

Artificial respiration: There are two methods of artificial respiration: chest compression and mouth-to-nose. Chest compression works by applying force to the chest wall, which pushes air out and allows the natural recoil of the chest to draw air in. It is the easiest to perform. Mouth-to-nose is forced respiration. It is used when the compression technique fails or when the chest is punctured.

To perform artificial respiration/chest compression:

1. Lay your dog on his right side and remove collar and harness.

2. Open your dog's mouth and check for possible obstructions.

3. Place both hands on the chest and press down sharply. Release quickly. If done properly, air should move in and out. If not, perform mouth-to-nose respiration.

4. Continue until your dog breathes on his own or as long as the heart beats.

To perform artificial respiration/mouth-to-nose:

1. Lay your dog on his right side and remove collar and harness.

2. Open your dog's mouth and check for possible obstructions.

3. Pull the tongue forward and close the mouth.

4. Place your mouth over your dog's nose and blow in steadily for three seconds. The chest will expand. Release and exhale.

5. Continue until your dog breathes on his own or as long as the heart beats.

Heart massage: Heart massage is used when there is no pulse, which often follows a cessation of breathing.

To perform:

1. Feel for pulse or heartbeat.

2. Open your dog's mouth and check for possible obstructions.

3. Lay your dog on her right side and remove collar and harness.

4. Place your thumb on one side of the sternum and fingers on the other side just below the elbows. For large dogs, place the heel of your hand on rib cage behind the elbow, which is directly over the heart.

5. With hands in this position, squeeze firmly to compress the chest. Do so five or six times. Wait five seconds to let the chest expand and repeat.

6. Continue until the heart beats on its own or until no pulse is felt for five minutes.

Combining heart massage and artificial respiration may require two people, one to massage and one to respirate. In an emergency situation where help is not available, after five cardiac massages perform one artificial (mouth-to-nose) respiration without breaking the rhythm or the massages.

Use a scarf or old hose to make a temporary muzzle, as shown.

Your Happy, Healthy Pet

Your Dog's Name _____

Name on Your Dog's Pedigree (if your dog has one) _____

_____

Where Your Dog Came From _____

_____

Your Dog's Birthday _____

Your Dog's Veterinarian

    Name _____

    Address _____

    Phone Number_____

    Emergency Number_____

Your Dog's Health

    Vaccines

    type _____ date given _____

    type _____ date given _____

    type _____ date given _____

    type _____ date given _____

    Heartworm

    date tested _____ type used_____ start date _____

Your Dog's License Number_____

Groomer's Name and Number _____

Dogsitter/Walker's Name and Number _____

Awards Your Dog Has Won

    Award _____ date earned _____

    Award _____ date earned _____

part three

Enjoying
your
Dog

chapter 8

Basic
Training

by Ian Dunbar, Ph.D., MRCVS

Training is the jewel in the crown—the most important aspect of doggy husbandry. There is no more important variable influencing dog behavior and temperament than the dog's education: A well-trained, well-behaved and good-natured puppydog is always a joy to live with, but an untrained and un-civilized dog can be a perpetual nightmare. Moreover, deny the dog an education and she will not have the opportunity to fulfill her own canine potential; neither will she have the ability to communicate effectively with her human companions.

Luckily, modern psychological training methods are easy, efficient, effective and, above all, considerably dog-friendly and user-friendly.

Doggy education is as simple as it is enjoyable. But before you can have a good time play-training with your new dog, you have to learn what to do and how to do it. There is no bigger variable influencing the success of dog training than the *owner's* experience and expertise. *Before you embark on the dog's education, you must first educate yourself.*

Basic Training for Owners

Ideally, basic owner training should begin well *before* you select your dog. Find out all you can about your chosen breed first, then master rudimentary training and handling skills. If you already have your puppy-dog, owner training is a dire emergency—the clock is ticking! Especially for puppies, the first few weeks at home are the most important and influential days in the dog's life. Indeed, the cause of most adolescent and adult problems may be traced back to the initial days the pup explores her new home. This is the time to establish the *status quo*—to teach the puppydog how you would like her to behave and so prevent otherwise quite predictable problems.

In addition to consulting breeders and breed books such as this one (which understandably have a positive breed bias), seek out as many pet owners with your breed as you can find. Good points are obvious. What you want to find out are the breed-specific *problems,* so you can nip them in the bud. In particular, you should talk to owners with *adolescent* dogs and make a list of all anticipated problems. Most important, *test drive* at least half a dozen adolescent and adult dogs of your breed yourself. An 8-week-old puppy is deceptively easy to handle, but she will acquire adult size, speed and strength in just four months, so you should learn now what to prepare for.

Puppy and pet dog training classes offer a convenient venue to locate pet owners and observe dogs in action. For a list of suitable trainers in your area, contact the Association of Pet Dog Trainers (see chapter 13). You may also begin your basic owner training by observing other owners in class. Watch as many classes and test drive as many dogs as possible. Select an upbeat, dog-friendly, people-friendly, fun-and-games, puppydog pet training class to learn the ropes. Also, watch training videos and read training books. You must find out what to do and how to do it *before* you have to do it.

Principles of Training

Most people think training comprises teaching the dog to do things such as sit, speak and roll over, but even a 4-week-old pup knows how to do these things already. Instead, the first step in training involves teaching the dog human words for each dog behavior and activity and for each aspect of the dog's environment. That way you, the owner, can more easily participate in the dog's domestic education by directing her to perform specific actions appropriately, that is, at the right time, in the right place and so on. Training opens communication channels, enabling an educated dog to at least understand her owner's requests.

In addition to teaching a dog *what* we want her to do, it is also necessary to teach her *why* she should do what we ask. Indeed, 95 percent of training revolves around motivating the dog *to want to do* what we want. Dogs often understand what their owners want; they just don't see the point of doing it—especially when the owner's repetitively boring and seemingly senseless instructions are totally at odds with much more pressing and exciting doggy distractions. It is not so much the dog that is being stubborn or dominant; rather, it is the owner who has failed to acknowledge the dog's needs and feelings and to approach training from the dog's point of view.

THE MEANING OF INSTRUCTIONS

The secret to successful training is learning how to use training lures to predict or prompt specific behaviors—to coax the dog to do what you want *when* you want. Any highly valued object (such as a treat or toy) may be used as a lure, which the dog will follow with her eyes and nose. Moving the lure in specific ways entices the dog to move her nose, head and entire body in specific ways. In fact, by learning the art of manipulating various lures, it is possible to teach the dog to assume virtually any body position and perform any action. Once you have control over the expression of the dog's behaviors and can elicit any body position or behavior at will, you can easily teach the dog to perform on request.

Teach your dog words for each activity she needs to know, like down.

Tell your dog what you want her to do, use a lure to entice her to respond correctly, then profusely praise and maybe reward her once she performs the desired action. For example, verbally request "Tina, sit!" while you move a squeaky toy upwards and backwards over the dog's muzzle (lure-movement and hand signal), smile knowingly as she looks up (to follow the lure) and sits down (as a result of canine anatomical engineering), then praise her to distraction ("Gooood Tina!"). Squeak the toy, offer a training treat and give your dog and yourself a pat on the back.

Being able to elicit desired responses over and over enables the owner to reward the dog over and over. Consequently, the dog begins to think training is fun. For example, the more the dog is rewarded for sitting, the more she enjoys sitting. Eventually the dog comes to realize that, whereas most sitting is appreciated, sitting immediately upon request usually prompts especially enthusiastic praise and a slew of high-level rewards. The dog begins to sit on cue much of the time, showing that she is starting to grasp the meaning of the owner's verbal request and hand signal.

WHY COMPLY?

Most dogs enjoy initial lure-reward training and are only too happy to comply with their owners' wishes. Unfortunately, repetitive drilling without appreciative feedback tends to diminish the dog's enthusiasm until she eventually fails to see the point of complying anymore. Moreover, as the dog approaches adolescence she becomes more easily distracted as she develops other interests. Lengthy sessions with repetitive exercises tend to bore and demotivate both parties. If it's not fun, the owner doesn't do it and neither does the dog.

Integrate training into your dog's life: The greater number of training sessions each day and the *shorter* they are, the more willingly compliant your dog will

To train your dog, you need gentle hands, a loving heart and a good attitude.

become. Make sure to have a short (just a few seconds) training interlude before every enjoyable canine activity. For example, ask your dog to sit to greet people, to sit before you throw her Frisbee and to sit for her supper. Really, sitting is no different from a canine "Please." Also, include numerous short training interludes during every enjoyable canine pastime, for example, when playing with the dog or when she is running in the park. In this fashion, doggy distractions may be effectively converted into rewards for training. Just as all games have rules, fun becomes training . . . and training becomes fun.

Eventually, rewards actually become unnecessary to continue motivating your dog. If trained with consideration and kindness, performing the desired behaviors will become self-rewarding and, in a sense, your dog will motivate herself. Just as it is not necessary to reward a human companion during an enjoyable walk in the park, or following a game of tennis, it is hardly necessary to reward our best friend—the dog— for walking by our side or while playing fetch. Human company during enjoyable activities is reward enough for most dogs.

Even though your dog has become self-motivating, it's still good to praise and pet her a lot and offer rewards once in a while, especially for a good job well done. And if for no other reason, praising and rewarding others is good for the human heart.

PUNISHMENT

Without a doubt, lure-reward training is by far the best way to teach: Entice your dog to do what you want and then reward her for doing so. Unfortunately, a human shortcoming is to take the good for granted and to moan and groan at the bad. Specifically, the dog's many good behaviors are ignored while the owner focuses on punishing the dog for making mistakes. In extreme cases, instruction is *limited* to punishing mistakes made by a trainee dog, child, employee or husband, even though it has been proven punishment training is notoriously inefficient and ineffective and is decidedly unfriendly and combative. It teaches the dog that training is a drag, almost as quickly as it teaches the dog to dislike her trainer. Why treat our best friends like our worst enemies?

Punishment training is also much more laborious and time consuming. Whereas it takes only a finite amount of time to teach a dog what to chew, for example, it takes much, much longer to punish the dog for each and every mistake. Remember, *there is only one right way!* So why not teach that right way from the outset?!

To make matters worse, punishment training causes severe lapses in the dog's reliability. Since it is obviously impossible to punish the dog each and every time she misbehaves, the dog quickly learns to distinguish between those times when she must comply (so as to avoid impending punishment) and those times when she need not comply, because punishment is impossible. Such times include when the dog is off leash and 6 feet away, when the owner is otherwise engaged (talking to a friend, watching television, taking a shower, tending to the baby or chatting on the telephone) or when the dog is left at home alone.

Instances of misbehavior will be numerous when the owner is away, because even when the dog complied in the owner's looming presence, she did so unwillingly. The dog was forced to act against her will, rather than molding her will to want to please. Hence, when the owner is absent, not only does the dog know she need not comply, she simply does not want to. Again, the trainee is not a stubborn vindictive beast, but rather the trainer has failed to teach. Punishment training invariably creates unpredictable Jekyll and Hyde behavior.

Trainer's Tools

Many training books extol the virtues of a vast array of training paraphernalia and electronic and metallic gizmos, most of which are designed for canine restraint, correction and punishment, rather than for actual facilitation of doggy education. In reality, most effective training tools are not found in stores; they come from within ourselves. In addition to a willing dog, all you really need is a functional human brain, gentle hands, a loving heart and a good attitude.

In terms of equipment, all dogs do require a quality buckle collar to sport dog tags and to attach the leash (for safety and to comply with local leash laws). Hollow chew toys (like Kongs or sterilized longbones) and a dog bed or collapsible crate are musts for housetraining. Three additional tools are required:

1. specific lures (training treats and toys) to predict and prompt specific desired behaviors;

2. rewards (praise, affection, training treats and toys) to reinforce for the dog what a lot of fun it all is; and

3. knowledge—how to convert the dog's favorite activities and games (potential distractions to training) into "life-rewards," which may be employed to facilitate training.

The most powerful of these is *knowledge*. Education is the key! Watch training classes, participate in training classes, watch videos, read books, enjoy play-training with your dog and then your dog will say "Please," and your dog will say "Thank you!"

Housetraining

If dogs were left to their own devices, certainly they would chew, dig and bark for entertainment and then no doubt highlight a few areas of their living space with sprinkles of urine, in much the same way we decorate by hanging pictures. Consequently, when we ask a dog to live with us, we must teach her *where* she may dig, *where* she may perform her toilet duties, *what* she may chew and *when* she may bark. After all, when left at home alone for many hours, we cannot expect the dog to amuse herself by completing crosswords or watching the soaps on TV!

Also, it would be decidedly unfair to keep the house rules a secret from the dog, and then get angry and punish the poor critter for inevitably transgressing rules she did not even know existed. Remember: Without adequate education and guidance, the dog will be forced to establish her own rules—doggy rules—and most probably will be at odds with the owner's view of domestic living.

Since most problems develop during the first few days the dog is at home, prospective dog owners must be certain they are quite clear about the principles of housetraining *before* they get a dog. Early misbehaviors quickly become established as the *status quo*—

becoming firmly entrenched as hard-to-break bad habits, which set the precedent for years to come. Make sure to teach your dog good habits right from the start. Good habits are just as hard to break as bad ones!

Ideally, when a new dog comes home, try to arrange for someone to be present as much as possible during the first few days (for adult dogs) or weeks for puppies. With only a little forethought, it is surprisingly easy to find a puppy sitter, such as a retired person, who would be willing to eat from your refrigerator and watch your television while keeping an eye on the newcomer to encourage the dog to play with chew toys and to ensure she goes outside on a regular basis.

POTTY TRAINING

To teach the dog where to relieve herself:

1. never let her make a single mistake;

2. let her know where you want her to go; and

3. handsomely reward her for doing so: "GOOOOOOOD DOG!!!" liver treat, liver treat, liver treat!

Preventing Mistakes

A single mistake is a training disaster, since it heralds many more in future weeks. And each time the dog soils the house, this further reinforces the dog's unfortunate preference for an indoor, carpeted toilet. *Do not let an unhousetrained dog have full run of the house.*

When you are away from home, or cannot pay full attention, confine the dog to an area where elimination is appropriate, such as an outdoor run or, better still, a small, comfortable indoor kennel with access to an outdoor run. When confined in this manner, most dogs will naturally housetrain themselves.

If that's not possible, confine the dog to an area, such as a utility room, kitchen, basement or garage, where elimination may not be desired in the long run but as an interim measure it is certainly preferable to doing it all around the house. Use newspaper to cover the floor of the dog's day room. The newspaper may be used to soak up the urine and to wrap up and dispose of the feces. Once your dog develops a preferred spot for eliminating, it is only necessary to cover that part of the floor with newspaper. The smaller papered area may then be moved (only a little each day) towards the door to the outside. Thus the dog will develop the tendency to go to the door when she needs to relieve herself.

Never confine an unhousetrained dog to a crate for long periods. Doing so would force the dog to soil the crate and ruin its usefulness as an aid for housetraining (see the following discussion).

Teaching Where

In order to teach your dog where you would like her to do her business, you have to be there to direct the proceedings—an obvious, yet often neglected, fact of life. In order to be there to teach the dog *where* to go, you need to know *when* she needs to go. Indeed, the success of housetraining depends on the owner's ability to predict these times. Certainly, a regular feeding schedule will facilitate prediction somewhat, but there is nothing like "loading the deck" and influencing the timing of the outcome yourself!

The first few weeks at home are the most important and influential in your dog's life.

Whenever you are at home, make sure the dog is under constant supervision and/or confined to a small area. If already well trained, simply instruct the dog to lie down in her bed or basket. Alternatively, confine the dog to a crate (doggy den) or tie-down (a short, 18-inch lead that can be clipped to an eye hook in the baseboard near her bed). Short-term close confinement strongly inhibits urination and defecation, since the dog does not want to soil her sleeping area. Thus, when you release the puppydog each hour, she will definitely need to urinate immediately and defecate every third or fourth hour. Keep the dog confined to her doggy den and take her to her intended toilet area each hour, every hour and on the hour.

When taking your dog outside, instruct her to sit quietly before opening the door—she will soon learn to sit by the door when she needs to go out!

Teaching Why

Being able to predict when the dog needs to go enables the owner to be on the spot to praise and reward the dog. Each hour, hurry the dog to the intended toilet area in the yard, issue the appropriate instruction ("Go pee!" or "Go poop!"), then give the dog three to four minutes to produce. Praise and offer a couple of training treats when successful. The treats are important because many people fail to praise their dogs with feeling . . . and housetraining is hardly the time for understatement. So either loosen up and enthusiastically praise that dog: "Wuzzzer-wuzzer-wuzzer, hoooser good wuffer den? Hoooo went pee for Daddy?" Or say "Good dog!" as best you can and offer the treats for effect.

Following elimination is an ideal time for a spot of play-training in the yard or house. Also, an empty dog may be allowed greater freedom around the house for the next half hour or so, just as long as you keep an eye out to make sure she does not get into other kinds of mischief. If you are preoccupied and cannot pay full attention, confine the dog to her doggy den once more to enjoy a peaceful snooze or to play with her many chew toys.

If your dog does not eliminate within the allotted time outside—no biggie! Back to her doggy den, and then try again after another hour.

As I own large dogs, I always feel more relaxed walking an empty dog, knowing that I will not need to finish our stroll weighted down with bags of feces!

Beware of falling into the trap of walking the dog to get her to eliminate. The good ol' dog walk is such an enormous highlight in the dog's life that it represents the single biggest potential reward in domestic dogdom. However, when in a hurry, or during inclement weather, many owners abruptly terminate the walk the moment the dog has done her business. This, in effect, severely punishes the dog for doing the right thing, in the right place at the right time. Consequently, many dogs become strongly inhibited from eliminating outdoors because they know it will signal an abrupt end to an otherwise thoroughly enjoyable walk.

Instead, instruct the dog to relieve herself in the yard prior to going for a walk. If you follow the above instructions, most dogs soon learn to eliminate on cue. As soon as the dog eliminates, praise (and offer a treat or two)—"Good dog! Let's go walkies!" Use the walk as a reward for eliminating in the yard. If the dog does not go, put her back in her doggy den and think about a walk later on. You will find with a "No feces—no walk" policy, your dog will become one of the fastest defecators in the business.

If you do not have a backyard, instruct the dog to eliminate right outside your front door prior to the walk. Not only will this facilitate clean up and disposal of the feces in your own trash can but, also, the walk may again be used as a colossal reward.

CHEWING AND BARKING

Short-term close confinement also teaches the dog that occasional quiet moments are a reality of domestic living. Your puppydog is extremely impressionable during her first few weeks at home. Regular confinement at this time soon exerts a calming influence over the dog's personality. Remember, once the dog is housetrained and calmer, there will be a whole lifetime ahead for the dog to enjoy full run of the house and garden. On the other hand, by letting the newcomer have unrestricted access to the entire household and allowing her to run willy-nilly, she will most certainly develop a bunch of behavior problems in short order, no doubt necessitating confinement later in life. It would not be fair to remedially restrain and confine a dog you have trained, through neglect, to run free.

When confining the dog, make sure she always has an impressive array of suitable chew toys. Kongs and sterilized longbones (both readily available from pet stores) make the best chew toys, since they are hollow and may be stuffed with treats to heighten the dog's interest. For example, by stuffing the little hole at the top of a Kong with a small piece of freeze-dried liver, the dog will not want to leave it alone.

Remember, treats do not have to be junk food and they certainly should not represent extra calories. Rather, treats should be part of each dog's regular

daily diet: Some food may be served in the dog's bowl for breakfast and dinner, some food may be used as training treats, and some food may be used for stuffing chew toys. I regularly stuff my dogs' many Kongs with different shaped biscuits and kibble.

Make sure your puppy has suitable chew toys.

The kibble seems to fall out fairly easily, as do the oval-shaped biscuits, thus rewarding the dog instantaneously for checking out the chew toys. The bone-shaped biscuits fall out after a while, rewarding the dog for worrying at the chew toy. But the triangular biscuits never come out. They remain inside the Kong as lures, maintaining the dog's fascination with her chew toy. To further focus the dog's interest, I always make sure to flavor the triangular biscuits by rubbing them with a little cheese or freeze-dried liver.

To teach come, call your dog, open your arms as a welcoming signal, wave a toy or a treat and praise for every step in your direction.

If stuffed chew toys are reserved especially for times the dog is confined, the puppydog will soon learn to enjoy quiet moments in her doggy den and she will quickly develop a chew-toy habit— a good habit! This is a simple *autoshaping* process; all the owner has to do is set up the situation and the dog all but trains herself— easy and effective. Even when the dog is given run of the house, her first inclination will be to indulge her rewarding chew-toy habit rather than destroy less-attractive household articles, such as curtains, carpets, chairs and compact disks. Similarly, a chew-toy chewer will be less inclined to scratch and chew herself excessively. Also, if the dog busies herself as a recreational chewer, she will be less inclined to develop into a recreational barker or digger when left at home alone.

Stuff a number of chew toys whenever the dog is left confined and remove the extra-special-tasting treats when you return. Your dog will now amuse herself with her chew toys before falling asleep and then resume playing with her chew toys when she expects you to return. Since most owner-absent misbehavior happens right after you leave and right before your expected return, your puppydog will now be conveniently preoccupied with her chew toys at these times.

Come and Sit

Most puppies will happily approach virtually anyone, whether called or not; that is, until they collide with adolescence and

develop other more important doggy interests, such as sniffing a multiplicity of exquisite odors on the grass. Your mission, Mr./Ms. Owner, is to teach and reward the pup for coming reliably, willingly and happily when called—and you have just three months to get it done. Unless adequately reinforced, your puppy's tendency to approach people will self-destruct by adolescence.

Call your dog ("Tina, come!"), open your arms (and maybe squat down) as a welcoming signal, waggle a treat or toy as a lure and reward the puppydog when she comes running. Do not wait to praise the dog until she reaches you—she may come 95 percent of the way and then run off after some distraction. Instead, praise the dog's *first* step towards you and continue praising enthusiastically for *every* step she takes in your direction.

When the rapidly approaching puppy dog is three lengths away from impact, instruct her to sit ("Tina, sit!") and hold the lure in front of you in an outstretched hand to prevent her from hitting you mid-chest and knocking you flat on your back! As Tina decelerates to nose the lure, move the treat upwards and backwards just over her muzzle with an upwards motion of your extended arm (palm-upwards). As the dog looks up to follow the lure, she will sit down (if she jumps up, you are holding the lure too high). Praise the dog for sitting. Move backwards and call her again. Repeat this many times over, always praising when Tina comes and sits; on occasion, reward her.

For the first couple of trials, use a training treat both as a lure to entice the dog to come and sit and as a reward for doing so. Thereafter, try to use different items as lures and rewards. For example, lure the dog with a Kong or Frisbee but reward her with a food treat. Or lure the dog with a food treat but pat her and throw a tennis ball as a reward. After just a few repetitions, dispense with the lures and rewards; the dog will begin to respond willingly to your verbal requests and hand signals just for the prospect of praise from your heart and affection from your hands.

Instruct every family member, friend and visitor how to get the dog to come and sit. Invite people over for a series of pooch parties; do not keep the pup a secret—let other people enjoy this puppy, and let the pup enjoy other people. Puppydog parties are not only fun, they easily attract a lot of people to help *you* train *your* dog. Unless you teach your dog how to meet people, that is, to sit for greetings, no doubt the dog will resort to jumping up. Then you and the visitors will get annoyed, and the dog will be punished. This is not fair. *Send out those invitations for puppy parties and teach your dog to be mannerly and socially acceptable.*

Even though your dog quickly masters obedient recalls in the house, her reliability may falter when playing in the backyard or local park. Ironically, it is *the owner* who has unintentionally trained the dog *not* to respond in these instances. By allowing the dog to play and run around and otherwise have a good time, but then to call the dog to put her on leash to take her home, the dog quickly learns playing is fun but training is a drag. Thus, playing in the park becomes a severe distraction, which works against training. Bad news!

Instead, whether playing with the dog off leash or on leash, request her to come at frequent intervals—say, every minute or so. On most occasions, praise and pet the dog for a few seconds while she is sitting, then tell her to go play again. For especially fast recalls, offer a couple of training treats and take the time to praise and pet the dog enthusiastically before releasing her. The dog will learn that coming when called is not necessarily the end of the play session, and neither is it the end of the world; rather, it signals an enjoyable, quality time-out with the owner before resuming play once more. In fact, playing in the park now becomes a very effective life-reward, which works to facilitate training by reinforcing each obedient and timely recall. Good news!

Sit, Down, Stand and Rollover

Teaching the dog a variety of body positions is easy for owner and dog, impressive for spectators and

Enjoying Your
Dog

extremely useful for all. Using lure-reward techniques, it is possible to train several positions at once to verbal commands or hand signals (which impress the socks off onlookers).

Sit and *down*—the two control commands—prevent or resolve nearly a hundred behavior problems. For example, if the dog happily and obediently sits or lies down when requested, she cannot jump on visitors, dash out the front door, run around and chase her tail, pester other dogs, harass cats or annoy family, friends or strangers. Additionally, "Sit" or "Down" are the best emergency commands for off-leash control.

It is easier to teach and maintain a reliable sit than maintain a reliable recall. *Sit* is the purest and simplest of commands—either the dog is sitting or she is not. If there is any change of circumstances or potential danger in the park, for example, simply instruct the dog to sit. If she sits, you have a number of options: Allow the dog to resume playing when she is safe, walk up and put the dog on leash or call the dog. The dog will be much more likely to come when called if she has already acknowledged her compliance by sitting. If the dog does not sit in the park—train her to!

Stand and *rollover-stay* are the two positions for examining the dog. Your veterinarian will love you to distraction if you take a little time to teach the dog to stand still and roll over and play possum. Also, your vet bills will be smaller because it will take the veterinarian less time to examine your dog. The rollover-stay is an especially useful command and is really just a variation of the down-stay: Whereas the dog lies prone in the traditional down, she lies supine in the rollover-stay.

As with teaching come and sit, the training techniques to teach the dog to assume all other body positions on cue are user-friendly and dog-friendly. Simply give the appropriate request, lure the dog into the desired body position using a training treat or toy and then *praise* (and maybe reward) the dog as soon as she complies. Try not to touch the dog to get her to respond. If you teach the dog by guiding her into position, the

114

dog will quickly learn that rump-pressure means sit, for example, but as yet you still have no control over your dog if she is just 6 feet away. It will still be necessary to teach the dog to sit on request. So do not make training a time-consuming two-step process; instead, teach the dog to sit to a verbal request or hand signal from the outset. Once the dog sits willingly when requested, by all means use your hands to pet the dog when she does so.

To teach *down* when the dog is already sitting, say "Tina, down!," hold the lure in one hand (palm down) and lower that hand to the floor between the dog's forepaws. As the dog lowers her head to follow the lure, slowly move the lure away from the dog just a fraction (in front of her paws). The dog will lie down as she stretches her nose forward to follow the lure. Praise the dog when she does so. If the dog stands up, you pulled the lure away too far and too quickly.

When teaching the dog to lie down from the standing position, say "Down" and lower the lure to the floor as before. Once the dog has lowered her forequarters and assumed a play bow, gently and slowly move the lure *towards* the dog between her forelegs. Praise the dog as soon as her rear end plops down.

After just a couple of trials it will be possible to alternate sits and downs and have the dog energetically perform doggy push-ups. Praise the dog a lot, and after half a dozen or so push-ups reward the dog with a training treat or toy. You will notice the more energetically you move your arm—upwards (palm up) to get the dog to sit, and downwards (palm down) to get the dog to lie down—the more energetically the dog responds to your requests. Now try training the dog in silence and you will notice she has also learned to respond to hand signals. Yeah! Not too shabby for the first session.

To teach *stand* from the sitting position, say "Tina, stand," slowly move the lure half a dog-length away from the dog's nose, keeping it at nose level, and praise the dog as she stands to follow the lure. As soon

115

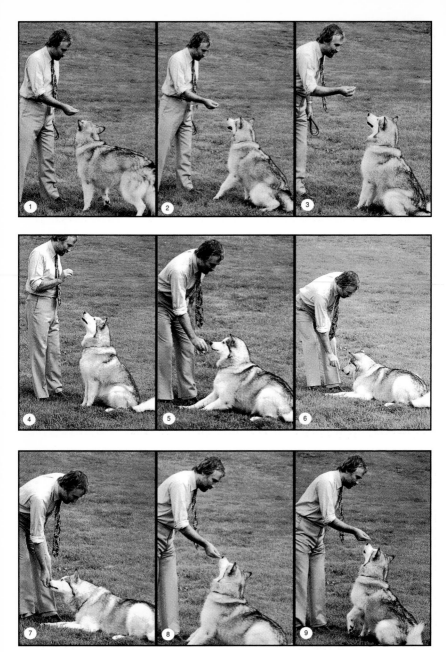

Using a food lure to teach sit, down and stand. 1) "Phoenix, sit." 2) Hand palm upwards, move lure up and back over dog's muzzle. 3) "Good sit, Phoenix!" 4) "Phoenix, down." 5) Hand palm downwards, move lure down to lie between dog's forepaws. 6) "Phoenix, off. Good down, Phoenix!" 7) "Phoenix, sit!" 8) Palm upwards, move lure up and back, keeping it close to dog's muzzle. 9) "Good sit, Phoenix!"

10) *"Phoenix, stand!"* 11) *Move lure away from dog at nose height, then lower it a tad.* 12) *"Phoenix, off! Good stand, Phoenix!"* 13) *"Phoenix, down!"* 14) *Hand palm downwards, move lure down to lie between dog's forepaws.* 15) *"Phoenix, off! Good down-stay, Phoenix!"* 16) *"Phoenix, stand!"* 17) *Move lure away from dog's muzzle up to nose height.* 18) *"Phoenix, off! Good stand-stay, Phoenix. Now we'll make the vet and groomer happy!"*

as the dog stands, lower the lure to just beneath the dog's chin to entice her to look down; otherwise she will stand and then sit immediately. To prompt the dog to stand from the down position, move the lure half a dog-length upwards and away from the dog, holding the lure at standing nose height from the floor.

Teaching *rollover* is best started from the down position, with the dog lying on one side, or at least with both hind legs stretched out on the same side. Say "Tina, bang!" and move the lure backwards and alongside the dog's muzzle to her elbow (on the side of her outstretched hind legs). Once the dog looks to the side and backwards, very slowly move the lure upwards to the dog's shoulder and backbone. Tickling the dog in the goolies (groin area) often invokes a reflex-raising of the hind leg as an appeasement gesture, which facilitates the tendency to roll over. If you move the lure too quickly and the dog jumps into the standing position, have patience and start again. As soon as the dog rolls onto her back, keep the lure stationary and mesmerize the dog with a relaxing tummy rub.

To teach *rollover-stay* when the dog is standing or moving, say "Tina, bang!" and give the appropriate hand signal (with index finger pointed and thumb cocked in true Sam Spade fashion), then in one fluid movement lure her to first lie down and then rollover-stay as above.

Teaching the dog to *stay* in each of the above four positions becomes a piece of cake after first teaching the dog not to worry at the toy or treat training lure. This is best accomplished by hand feeding dinner kibble. Hold a piece of kibble firmly in your hand and softly instruct "Off!" Ignore any licking and slobbering *for however long the dog worries at the treat*, but say "Take it!" and offer the kibble *the instant* the dog breaks contact with her muzzle. Repeat this a few times, and then up the ante and insist the dog remove her muzzle for one whole second before offering the kibble. Then progressively refine your criteria and have the dog not touch your hand (or treat) for longer and longer periods on each trial, such as for two seconds, four seconds, then six, ten, fifteen, twenty, thirty seconds and so on.

The dog soon learns: (1) worrying at the treat never gets results, whereas (2) noncontact is often rewarded after a variable time lapse.

Teaching *"Off!"* has many useful applications in its own right. Additionally, instructing the dog not to touch a training lure often produces spontaneous and magical stays. Request the dog to stand-stay, for example, and not to touch the lure. At first set your sights on a short two-second stay before rewarding the dog. (Remember, every long journey begins with a single step.) However, on subsequent trials, gradually and progressively increase the length of stay required to receive a reward. In no time at all your dog will stand calmly for a minute or so.

Relevancy Training

Once you have taught the dog what you expect her to do when requested to come, sit, lie down, stand, rollover and stay, the time is right to teach the dog *why* she should comply with your wishes. The secret is to have many (*many*) extremely short training interludes (two to five seconds each) at numerous (*numerous*) times during the course of the dog's day. Especially work with the dog immediately *before* the dog's good times and *during* the dog's good times. For example, ask your dog to sit and/or lie down each time before opening doors, serving meals, offering treats and tummy rubs; ask the dog to perform a few controlled doggy push-ups before letting her off leash or throwing a tennis ball; and perhaps request the dog to sit-down-sit-stand-down-stand-rollover before inviting her to cuddle on the couch.

Similarly, request the dog to sit many times during play or on walks, and in no time at all the dog will be only too pleased to follow your instructions because she has learned that a compliant response heralds all sorts of goodies. Basically all you are trying to teach the dog is how to say please: "Please throw the tennis ball. Please may I snuggle on the couch."

Remember, it is important to keep training interludes short and to have many short sessions each and every day. The shortest (and most useful) session comprises asking the dog to sit and then go play during a play session. When trained this way, your dog will soon associate training with good times. In fact, the dog may be unable to distinguish between training and good times and, indeed, there should be no distinction. The warped concept that training involves forcing the dog to comply and/or dominating her will is totally at odds with the picture of a truly well-trained dog. In reality, enjoying a game of training with a dog is no different from enjoying a game of backgammon or tennis with a friend; and walking with a dog should be no different from strolling with a spouse, or with buddies on the golf course.

Walk by Your Side

Many people attempt to teach a dog to heel by putting her on a leash and physically correcting the dog when she makes mistakes. There are a number of things seriously wrong with this approach, the first being that most people do not want precision heeling; rather, they simply want the dog to follow or walk by their side. Second, when physically restrained during "training," even though the dog may grudgingly mope by your side when "handcuffed" on leash, let's see what happens when she is off leash. History! The dog is in the next county because she never enjoyed walking with you on leash and you have no control over her off leash. So let's just teach the dog off leash from the outset to *want* to walk with us. Third, if the dog has not been trained to heel, it is a trifle hasty to think about punishing the poor dog for making mistakes and breaking heeling rules she didn't even know existed. This is simply not fair! Surely, if the dog had been adequately taught how to heel, she would seldom make mistakes and hence there would be no need to correct the dog. Remember, each mistake and each correction (punishment) advertise the trainer's inadequacy, not the dog's. The dog is not stubborn, she is not stupid and she is not bad. Even if she were, she would still require training, so let's train her properly.

Let's teach the dog to *enjoy* following us and to *want* to walk by our side off leash. Then it will be easier to teach high-precision off-leash heeling patterns if desired. Before going on outdoor walks, it is necessary to teach the dog not to pull. Then it becomes easy to teach on-leash walking and heeling because the dog already wants to walk with you, she is familiar with the desired walking and heeling positions and she knows not to pull.

FOLLOWING

Start by training your dog to follow you. Many puppies will follow if you simply walk away from them and maybe click your fingers or chuckle. Adult dogs may require additional enticement to stimulate them to follow, such as a training lure or, at the very least, a lively trainer. To teach the dog to follow: (1) keep walking and (2) walk away from the dog. If the dog attempts to lead or lag, change pace; slow down if the dog forges too far ahead, but speed up if she lags too far behind. Say "Steady!" or "Easy!" each time before you slow down and "Quickly!" or "Hustle!" each time before you speed up, and the dog will learn to change pace on cue. If the dog lags or leads too far, or if she wanders right or left, simply walk quickly in the opposite direction and maybe even run away from the dog and hide.

Practicing is a lot of fun; you can set up a course in your home, yard or park to do this. Indoors, entice the dog to follow upstairs, into a bedroom, into the bathroom, downstairs, around the living room couch, zigzagging between dining room chairs and into the kitchen for dinner. Outdoors, get the dog to follow around park benches, trees, shrubs and along walkways and lines in the grass. (For safety outdoors, it is advisable to attach a long line on the dog, but never exert corrective tension on the line.)

Remember, following has a lot to do with attitude—
your attitude! Most probably your dog will *not* want to
follow Mr. Grumpy Troll with the personality of wilted
lettuce. Lighten up—walk with a jaunty step, whistle a
happy tune, sing, skip and tell jokes to your dog and
she will be right there by your side.

BY YOUR SIDE

It is smart to train the dog to walk close on one side or
the other—either side will do, your choice. When walking, jogging or cycling, it is generally bad news to have
the dog suddenly cut in front of you. In fact, I train my
dogs to walk "By my side" and "Other side"—both very
useful instructions. It is possible to position the dog
fairly accurately by looking to the appropriate side and
clicking your fingers or slapping your thigh on that
side. A precise positioning may be attained by holding
a training lure, such as a chew toy, tennis ball or food
treat. Stop and stand still several times throughout the
walk, just as you would when window shopping or
meeting a friend. Use the lure to make sure the dog
slows down and stays close whenever you stop.

When teaching the dog to heel, we generally want
her to sit in heel position when we stop. Teach heel

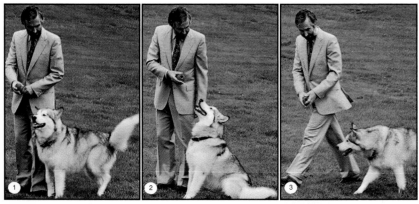

*Using a toy to teach sit-heel-sit sequences: 1) "Phoenix, sit!" Standing still, move lure up and back over dog's
muzzle . . . 2) to position dog sitting in heel position on your left side. 3) Say "Phoenix, heel!" and walk ahead,
wagging lure in left hand. Change lure to right hand in preparation for sit signal. Say "Sit" and then . . .*

position at the standstill and the dog will learn that the default heel position is sitting by your side (left or right—your choice, unless you wish to compete in obedience trials, in which case the dog must heel on the left).

Several times a day, stand up and call your dog to come and sit in heel position—"Tina, heel!" For example, instruct the dog to come to heel each time there are commercials on TV, or each time you turn a page of a novel, and the dog will get it in a single evening.

Practice straight-line heeling and turns separately. With the dog sitting at heel, teach her to turn in place. After each quarter-turn, half-turn or full turn in place, lure the dog to sit at heel. Now it's time for short straight-line heeling sequences, no more than a few steps at a time. Always think of heeling in terms of sit-heel-sit sequences—start and end with the dog in position and do your best to keep her there when moving. Progressively increase the number of steps in each sequence. When the dog remains close for 20 yards of straight-line heeling, it is time to add a few turns and then sign up for a happy-heeling obedience class to get some advice from the experts.

4) use hand signal to lure dog to sit as you stop. Eventually, dog will sit automatically at heel whenever you stop. 5) "Good dog!"

No Pulling on Leash

You can start teaching your dog not to pull on leash anywhere—in front of the television or outdoors—but regardless of location, you must not take a single step with tension in the leash. For a reason known only to dogs, even just a couple of paces of pulling on leash is intrinsically motivating and diabolically rewarding. Instead, attach the leash to the dog's collar, grasp the other end firmly with both hands held close to your chest, and stand still—do not budge an inch. Have somebody watch you with a stopwatch to time your progress, or else you will never believe this will work and so you will not even try the exercise, and your shoulder and the dog's neck will be traumatized for years to come.

Stand still and wait for the dog to stop pulling, and to sit and/or lie down. All dogs stop pulling and sit eventually. Most take only a couple of minutes; the all-time record is 22½ minutes. Time how long it takes. Gently praise the dog when she stops pulling, and as soon as she sits, enthusiastically praise the dog and take just one step forward, then immediately stand still. This single step usually demonstrates the ballistic reinforcing nature of pulling on leash; most dogs explode to the end of the leash, so be prepared for the strain. Stand firm and wait for the dog to sit again. Repeat this half a dozen times and you will probably notice a progressive reduction in the force of the dog's one-step explosions and a radical reduction in the time it takes for the dog to sit each time.

As the dog learns "Sit we go" and "Pull we stop," she will begin to walk forward calmly with each single step and automatically sit when you stop. Now try two steps before you stop. Wooooooo! Scary! When the dog has mastered two steps at a time, try for three. After each success, progressively increase the number of steps in the sequence: try four steps and then six, eight, ten and twenty steps before stopping. Congratulations! You are now walking the dog on leash.

Whenever walking with the dog (off leash or on leash), make sure you stop periodically to practice a few position commands and stays before instructing the dog to "Walk on!" (Remember, you want the dog to be compliant everywhere, not just in the kitchen when her dinner is at hand.) For example, stopping every 25 yards to briefly train the dog amounts to over 200 training interludes within a single 3-mile stroll. And each training session is in a different location. You will not believe the improvement within just the first mile of the first walk.

To put it another way, integrating training into a walk offers 200 separate opportunities to use the continuance of the walk as a reward to reinforce the dog's education. Moreover, some training interludes may comprise continuing education for the dog's walking skills: Alternate short periods of the dog walking calmly by your side with periods when the dog is allowed to sniff and investigate the environment. Now sniffing odors on the grass and meeting other dogs become rewards which reinforce the dog's calm and mannerly demeanor. Good Lord! Whatever next? Many enjoyable walks together of course. Happy trails!

THE IMPORTANCE OF TRICKS

Nothing will improve a dog's quality of life better than having a few tricks under her belt. Teaching any trick expands the dog's vocabulary, which facilitates communication and improves the owner's control. Also, specific tricks help prevent and resolve specific behavior problems. For example, by teaching the dog to fetch her toys, the dog learns carrying a toy makes the owner happy and, therefore, will be more likely to chew her toy than other inappropriate items.

More important, teaching tricks prompts owners to lighten up and train with a sunny disposition. Really, tricks should be no different from any other behaviors we put on cue. But they are. When teaching tricks, owners have a much sweeter attitude, which in turn motivates the dog and improves her willingness to comply. The dog feels tricks are a blast, but formal commands are a drag. In fact, tricks are so enjoyable, they may be used as rewards in training by asking the dog to come, sit and down-stay and then rollover for a tummy rub. Go on, try it: Crack a smile and even giggle when the dog promptly and willingly lies down and stays.

Most important, performing tricks prompts onlookers to smile and giggle. Many people are scared of dogs, especially large ones. And nothing can be more off-putting for a dog than to be constantly confronted by strangers who don't like her because of her size or the way she looks. Uneasy people put the dog on edge, causing her to back off and bark, only frightening people all the more. And so a vicious circle develops, with the people's fear fueling the dog's fear *and vice versa.* Instead, tie a pink ribbon to your dog's collar and practice all sorts of tricks on walks and in the park, and you will be pleasantly amazed how it changes people's attitudes toward your friendly dog. The dog's repertoire of tricks is limited only by the trainer's imagination. Below I have described three of my favorites:

SPEAK AND SHUSH

The training sequence involved in teaching a dog to bark on request is no different from that used when training any behavior on cue: request—lure—response—reward. As always, the secret of success lies in finding an effective lure. If the dog always barks at the doorbell, for example, say "Rover, speak!", have an accomplice ring the doorbell, then reward the dog for barking. After a few woofs, ask Rover to "Shush!", waggle a food treat under her nose (to entice her to sniff and thus to shush), praise her when quiet and eventually offer the treat as a reward. Alternate "Speak" and "Shush," progressively increasing the length of shush-time between each barking bout.

PLAY BOW

With the dog standing, say "Bow!" and lower the food lure (palm upwards) to rest between the dog's forepaws. Praise as the dog lowers

---

her forequarters and sternum to the ground (as when teaching the down), but then lure the dog to stand and offer the treat. On successive trials, gradually increase the length of time the dog is required to remain in the play bow posture in order to gain a food reward. If the dog's rear end collapses into a down, say nothing and offer no reward; simply start over.

BE A BEAR

With the dog sitting backed into a corner to prevent her from toppling over backwards, say "Be a bear!" With bent paw and palm down, raise a lure upwards and backwards along the top of the dog's muzzle. Praise the dog when she sits up on her haunches and offer the treat as a reward. To prevent the dog from standing on her hind legs, keep the lure closer to the dog's muzzle. On each trial, progressively increase the length of time the dog is required to sit up to receive a food reward. Since lure-reward training is so easy, teach the dog to stand and walk on her hind legs as well!

Teaching "Be a Bear"

chapter 9

Getting
Active
with your Dog

by Bardi McLennan

Once you and your dog have graduated from basic obedience training and are beginning to work together as a team, you can take part in the growing world of dog activities. There are so many fun things to do with your dog! Just remember, people and dogs don't always learn at the same pace, so don't be upset if you (or your dog) need more than two basic training courses before your team becomes operational. Even smart dogs don't go straight to college from kindergarten!

Just as there are events geared to certain types of dogs, so there are ones that are more appealing to certain types of people. In some

128

activities, you give the commands and your dog does the work (upland game hunting is one example), while in others, such as agility, you'll both get a work-out. You may want to aim for prestigious titles to add to your dog's name, or you may want nothing more than the sheer enjoyment of being around other people and their dogs. Passive or active, participation has its own rewards.

Consider your dog's physical capabilities when looking into any of the canine activities. It's easy to see that a Basset Hound is not built for the racetrack, nor would a Chihuahua be the breed of choice for pulling a sled. A loyal dog will attempt almost anything you ask him to do, so it is up to you to know your dog's limitations. A dog must be physically sound in order to compete at any level in athletic activities, and being mentally sound is a definite plus. Advanced age, however, may not be a deterrent. Many dogs still hunt and herd at ten or twelve years of age. It's entirely possible for dogs to be "fit at 50." Take your dog for a checkup, explain to your vet the type of activity you have in mind and be guided by his or her findings.

All dogs seem to love playing flyball.

You needn't be restricted to breed-specific sports if it's only fun you're after. Certain AKC activities are limited to designated breeds; however, as each new trial, test or sport has grown in popularity, so has the variety of breeds encouraged to participate at a fun level.

But don't shortchange your fun, or that of your dog, by thinking only of the basic function of her breed. Once a dog has learned how to learn, she can be taught to do just about anything as long as the size of the dog is right for the job and you both think it is fun and rewarding. In other words, you are a team.

To get involved in any of the activities detailed in this chapter, look for the names and addresses of the organizations that sponsor them in Chapter 13. You can also ask your breeder or a local dog trainer for contacts.

You can compete in obedience trials with a well trained dog.

Official American Kennel Club Activities

The following tests and trials are some of the events sanctioned by the AKC and sponsored by various dog clubs. Your dog's expertise will be rewarded with impressive titles. You can participate just for fun, or be competitive and go for those awards.

OBEDIENCE

Training classes begin with pups as young as three months of age in kindergarten puppy training, then advance to pre-novice (all exercises on lead) and go on to novice, which is where you'll start off-lead work. In obedience classes dogs learn to sit, stay, heel and come through a variety of exercises. Once you've got the basics down, you can enter obedience trials and work toward earning your dog's first degree, a C.D. (Companion Dog).

The next level is called "Open," in which jumps and retrieves perk up the dog's interest. Passing grades in competition at this level earn a C.D.X. (Companion Dog Excellent). Beyond that lies the goal of the most ambitious—Utility (U.D. and even U.D.X. or OTCh, an Obedience Champion).

AGILITY

All dogs can participate in the latest canine sport to have gained worldwide popularity for its fun and excitement, agility. It began in England as a canine version of horse show-jumping, but because dogs are more agile and able to perform on verbal commands, extra feats were added such as climbing, balancing and racing through tunnels or in and out of weave poles. Many of the obstacles (regulation or homemade) can be set up in your own backyard. If the agility bug bites, you could end up in international competition!

For starters, your dog should be obedience trained, even though, in the beginning, the lessons may all be taught on lead. Once the dog understands the commands (and you do, too), it's as easy as guiding the dog over a prescribed course, one obstacle at a time. In competition, the race is against the clock, so wear your running shoes! The dog starts with 200 points and the judge deducts for infractions and misadventures along the way.

All dogs seem to love agility and respond to it as if they were being turned loose in a playground paradise. Your dog's enthusiasm will be contagious; agility turns into great fun for dog and owner.

FIELD TRIALS AND HUNTING TESTS

There are field trials and hunting tests for the sporting breeds—retrievers, spaniels and pointing breeds, and for some hounds—Bassets, Beagles and Dachshunds. Field trials are competitive events that test a dog's ability to perform the functions for which she was bred. Hunting tests, which are open to retrievers,

---

TITLES AWARDED BY THE AKC

Conformation: Ch. (Champion)

Obedience: CD (Companion Dog); CDX (Companion Dog Excellent); UD (Utility Dog); UDX (Utility Dog Excellent); OTCh. (Obedience Trial Champion)

Field: JH (Junior Hunter); SH (Senior Hunter); MH (Master Hunter); AFCh. (Amateur Field Champion); FCh. (Field Champion)

Lure Coursing: JC (Junior Courser); SC (Senior Courser)

Herding: HT (Herding Tested); PT (Pre-Trial Tested); HS (Herding Started); HI (Herding Intermediate); HX (Herding Excellent); HCh. (Herding Champion)

Tracking: TD (Tracking Dog); TDX (Tracking Dog Excellent)

Agility: NAD (Novice Agility); OAD (Open Agility); ADX (Agility Excellent); MAX (Master Agility)

Earthdog Tests: JE (Junior Earthdog); SE (Senior Earthdog); ME (Master Earthdog)

Canine Good Citizen: CGC

Combination: DC (Dual Champion—Ch. and FCh.); TC (Triple Champion—Ch., FCh., and OTCh.)

---

spaniels and pointing breeds only, are noncompetitive and are a means of judging the dog's ability as well as that of the handler.

Hunting is a very large and complex part of canine sports, and if you own one of the breeds that hunts, the events are a great treat for your dog and you. He gets to do what he was bred for, and you get to work with him and watch him do it. You'll be proud of and amazed at what your dog can do.

Fortunately, the AKC publishes a series of booklets on these events, which outline the rules and regulations and include a glossary of the sometimes complicated terms. The AKC also publishes newsletters for field trialers and hunting test enthusiasts. The United Kennel Club (UKC) also has informative materials for the hunter and his dog.

Retrievers and other sporting breeds get to do what they're bred to in hunting tests.

HERDING TESTS AND TRIALS

Herding, like hunting, dates back to the first known uses man made of dogs. The interest in herding today is widespread, and if you own a herding breed, you can join in the activity. Herding dogs are tested for their natural skills to keep a flock of ducks, sheep or cattle together. If your dog shows potential, you can start at the testing level, where your dog can earn a title for showing an inherent herding ability. With training you can advance to the trial level, where your dog should be capable of controlling even difficult livestock in diverse situations.

LURE COURSING

The AKC Tests and Trials for Lure Coursing are open to traditional sighthounds—Greyhounds, Whippets,

Borzoi, Salukis, Afghan Hounds, Ibizan Hounds and Scottish Deerhounds—as well as to Basenjis and Rhodesian Ridgebacks. Hounds are judged on overall ability, follow, speed, agility and endurance. This is possibly the most exciting of the trials for spectators, because the speed and agility of the dogs is awesome to watch as they chase the lure (or "course") in heats of two or three dogs at a time.

TRACKING

Tracking is another activity in which almost any dog can compete because every dog that sniffs the ground when taken outdoors is, in fact, tracking. The hard part comes when the rules as to what, when and where the dog tracks are determined by a person, not the dog! Tracking tests cover a large area of fields, woods and roads. The tracks are laid hours before the dogs go to work on them, and include "tricks" like cross-tracks and sharp turns. If you're interested in search-and-rescue work, this is the place to start.

This tracking dog is hot on the trail.

EARTHDOG TESTS FOR SMALL TERRIERS AND DACHSHUNDS

These tests are open to Australian, Bedlington, Border, Cairn, Dandie Dinmont, Smooth and Wire Fox, Lakeland, Norfolk, Norwich, Scottish, Sealyham, Skye, Welsh and West Highland White Terriers as well as Dachshunds. The dogs need no prior training for this terrier sport. There is a qualifying test on the day of the event, so dog and handler learn the rules on the spot. These tests, or "digs," sometimes end with informal races in the late afternoon.

Here are some of the extracurricular obedience and racing activities that are not regulated by the AKC or UKC, but are generally run by clubs or a group of dog fanciers and are often open to all.

Canine Freestyle This activity is something new on the scene and is variously likened to dancing, dressage or ice skating. It is meant to show the athleticism of the dog, but also requires showmanship on the part of the dog's handler. If you and your dog like to ham it up for friends, you might want to look into freestyle.

Lure coursing lets sighthounds do what they do best—run!

Scent Hurdle Racing Scent hurdle racing is purely a fun activity sponsored by obedience clubs with members forming competing teams. The height of the hurdles is based on the size of the shortest dog on the team. On a signal, one team dog is released on each of two side-by-side courses and must clear every hurdle before picking up its own dumbbell from a platform and returning over the jumps to the handler. As each dog returns, the next on that team is sent. Of course, that is what the dogs are supposed to do. When the dogs improvise (going under or around the hurdles, stealing another dog's dumbbell, and so forth), it no doubt frustrates the handlers, but just adds to the fun for everyone else.

Flyball This type of racing is similar, but after negotiating the four hurdles, the dog comes to a flyball box, steps on a lever that releases a tennis ball into the air, catches the ball and returns over the hurdles to the starting point. This game also becomes extremely fun for spectators because the dogs sometimes cheat by catching a ball released by the dog in the next lane. Three titles can be earned—Flyball Dog (F.D.), Flyball Dog Excellent (F.D.X.) and Flyball Dog Champion (Fb.D.Ch.)—all awarded by the North American Flyball Association, Inc.

Dogsledding The name conjures up the Rocky Mountains or the frigid North, but you can find dogsled clubs in such unlikely spots as Maryland, North Carolina and Virginia! Dogsledding is primarily for the Nordic breeds such as the Alaskan Malamutes, Siberian Huskies and Samoyeds, but other breeds can try. There are some practical backyard applications to this sport, too. With parental supervision, almost any strong dog could pull a child's sled.

Coming over the A-frame on an agility course.

These are just some of the many recreational ways you can get to know and understand your multifaceted dog better and have fun doing it.

chapter 10

Your Dog
and your
Family

by Bardi McLennan

Adding a dog automatically increases your family by one, no matter whether you live alone in an apartment or are part of a mother, father and six kids household. The single-person family is fair game for numerous and varied canine misconceptions as to who is dog and who pays the bills, whereas a dog in a houseful of children will consider himself to be just one of the gang, littermates all. One dog and one child may give a dog reason to believe they are both kids or both dogs.

Either interpretation requires parental supervision and sometimes speedy intervention.

As soon as one paw goes through the door into your home, Rufus (or Rufina) has to make many adjustments to become a part of your family. Your job is to make him fit in as painlessly as possible. An older dog may have some frame of reference from past experience, but to a 10-week-old puppy, everything is brand new: people, furniture, stairs, when and where people eat, sleep or watch TV, his own place and everyone else's space, smells, sounds, outdoors—everything!

Puppies, and newly acquired dogs of any age, do not need what we think of as "freedom." If you leave a new dog or puppy loose in the house, you will almost certainly return to chaotic destruction and the dog will forever after equate your homecoming with a time of punishment to be dreaded. It is unfair to give your dog what amounts to "freedom to get into trouble." Instead, confine him to a crate for brief periods of your absence (up to

Lots of pets get along with each other just fine.

three or four hours) and, for the long haul, a workday for example, confine him to one untrashable area with his own toys, a bowl of water and a radio left on (low) in another room.

For the first few days, when not confined, put Rufus on a long leash tied to your wrist or waist. This umbilical cord method enables the dog to learn all about you from your body language and voice, and to learn by his own actions which things in the house are NO! and which ones are rewarded by "Good dog." House-training will be easier with the pup always by your side. Speaking of which, accidents do happen. That goal of "completely housetrained" takes up to a year, or the length of time it takes the pup to mature.

The All-Adult Family

Most dogs in an adults-only household today are likely to be latchkey pets, with no one home all day but the

137

dog. When you return after a tough day on the job, the dog can and should be your relaxation therapy. But going home can instead be a daily frustration.

Separation anxiety is a very common problem for the dog in a working household. It may begin with whines and barks of loneliness, but it will soon escalate into a frenzied destruction derby. That is why it is so important to set aside the time to teach a dog to relax when left alone in his confined area and to understand that he can trust you to return.

Let the dog get used to your work schedule in easy stages. Confine him to one room and go in and out of that room over and over again. Be casual about it. No physical, voice or eye contact. When the pup no longer even notices your comings and goings, leave the house for varying lengths of time, returning to stay home for a few minutes and gradually increasing the time away. This training can take days, but the dog is learning that you haven't left him forever and that he can trust you.

Any time you leave the dog, but especially during this training period, be casual about your departure. No anxiety-building fond farewells. Just "Bye" and go! Remember the "Good dog" when you return to find everything more or less as you left it.

If things are a mess (or even a disaster) when you return, greet the dog, take him outside to eliminate, and then put him in his crate while you clean up. Rant and rave in the shower! *Do not* punish the dog. You were not there when it happened, and the rule is: Only punish as you catch the dog in the act of wrongdoing. Obviously, it makes sense to get your latchkey puppy when you'll have a week or two to spend on these training essentials.

Family weekend activities should include Rufus whenever possible. Depending on the pup's age, now is the time for a long walk in the park, playtime in the backyard, a hike in the woods. Socializing is as important as health care, good food and physical exercise, so visiting Aunt Emma or Uncle Harry and the next-door neighbor's dog or cat is essential to developing an outgoing, friendly temperament in your pet.

If you are a single adult, socializing Rufus at home and away will prevent him from becoming overly protective of you (or just overly attached) and will also prevent such behavioral problems as dominance or fear of strangers.

Babies

Whether already here or on the way, babies figure larger than life in the eyes of a dog. If the dog is there first, let him in on all your baby preparations in the house. When baby arrives, let Rufus sniff any item of clothing that has been on the baby before Junior comes home. Then let Mom greet the dog first before introducing the new family member. Hold the baby down for the dog to see and sniff, but make sure someone's holding the dog on lead in case of any sudden moves. Don't play keep-away or tease the dog with the baby, which only invites undesirable jumping up.

The dog and the baby are "family," and for starters can be treated almost as equals. Things rapidly change, however, especially when baby takes to creeping around on all fours on the dog's turf or, better yet, has yummy pudding all over her face and hands! That's when a lot of things in the dog's and baby's lives become more separate than equal.

Dogs are perfect confidants.

Toddlers make terrible dog owners, but if you can't avoid the combination, use patient discipline (that is, positive teaching rather than punishment), and use time-outs before you run out of patience.

A dog and a baby (or toddler, or an assertive young child) should never be left alone together. Take the dog with you or confine him. With a baby or youngsters in the house, you'll have plenty of use for that wonderful canine safety device called a crate!

Young Children

Any dog in a house with kids will behave pretty much as the kids do, good or bad. But even good dogs and good children can get into trouble when play becomes rowdy and active.

Teach children how to play nicely with a puppy.

Legs bobbing up and down, shrill voices screeching, a ball hurtling overhead, all add up to exuberant frustration for a dog who's just trying to be part of the gang. In a pack of puppies, any legs or toys being chased would be caught by a set of teeth, and all the pups involved would understand that is how the game is played. Kids do not understand this, nor do parents tolerate it. Bring Rufus indoors before you have reason to regret it. This is time-out, not a punishment.

You can explain the situation to the children and tell them they must play quieter games until the puppy learns not to grab them with his mouth. Unfortunately, you can't explain it that easily to the dog. With adult supervision, they will learn how to play together.

Young children love to tease. Sticking their faces or wiggling their hands or fingers in the dog's face is teasing. To another person it might be just annoying, but it is threatening to a dog. There's another difference: We can make the child stop by an explanation, but the only way a dog can stop it is with a warning growl and then with teeth. Teasing is the major cause of children being bitten by their pets. Treat it seriously.

140

Older Children

The best age for a child to get a first dog is between the ages of 8 and 12. That's when kids are able to accept some real responsibility for their pet. Even so, take the child's vow of "I will never *ever* forget to feed (brush, walk, etc.) the dog" for what it's worth: a child's good intention at that moment. Most kids today have extra lessons, soccer practice, Little League, ballet, and so forth piled on top of school schedules. There will be many times when Mom will have to come to the dog's rescue. "I walked the dog for you so you can set the table for me" is one way to get around a missed appointment without laying on blame or guilt.

Kids in this age group make excellent obedience trainers because they are into the teaching/learning process themselves and they lack the self-consciousness of adults. Attending a dog show is something the whole family can enjoy, and watching Junior Showmanship may catch the eye of the kids. Older children can begin to get involved in many of the recreational activities that were reviewed in the previous chapter. Some of the agility obstacles, for example, can be set up in the backyard as a family project (with an adult making sure all the equipment is safe and secure for the dog).

Older kids are also beginning to look to the future, and may envision themselves as veterinarians or trainers or show dog handlers or writers of the next Lassie best-seller. Dogs are perfect confidants for these dreams. They won't tell a soul.

Other Pets

Introduce all pets tactfully. In a dog/cat situation, hold the dog, not the cat. Let two dogs meet on neutral turf—a stroll in the park or a walk down the street—with both on loose leads to permit all the normal canine ways of saying hello, including routine sniffing, circling, more sniffing, and so on. Small creatures such as hamsters, chinchillas or mice must be kept safe from their natural predators (dogs and cats).

Festive Family Occasions

Parties are great for people, but not necessarily for puppies. Until all the guests have arrived, put the dog in his crate or in a room where he won't be disturbed. A socialized dog can join the fun later as long as he's not underfoot, annoying guests or into the hors d'oeuvres.

There are a few dangers to consider, too. Doors opening and closing can allow a puppy to slip out unnoticed in the confusion, and you'll be organizing a search party instead of playing host or hostess. Party food and buffet service are not for dogs. Let Rufus party in his crate with a nice big dog biscuit.

At Christmas time, not only are tree decorations dangerous and breakable (and perhaps family heirlooms), but extreme caution should be taken with the lights, cords and outlets for the tree lights and any other festive lighting. Occasionally a dog lifts a leg, ignoring the fact that the tree is indoors. To avoid this, use a canine repellent, made for gardens, on the tree. Or keep him out of the tree room unless supervised. And whatever you do, *don't* invite trouble by hanging his toys on the tree!

Car Travel

Before you plan a vacation by car or RV with Rufus, be sure he enjoys car travel. Nothing spoils a holiday quicker than a carsick dog! Work within the dog's comfort level. Get in the car with the dog in his crate or attached to a canine car safety belt and just sit there until he relaxes. That's all. Next time, get in the car, turn on the engine and go nowhere. Just sit. When that is okay, turn on the engine and go around the block. Now you can go for a ride and include a stop where you get out, leaving the dog for a minute or two.

On a warm day, always park in the shade and leave windows open several inches. And return quickly. It only takes 10 minutes for a car to become an overheated steel death trap.

Motel or Pet Motel?

Not all motels or hotels accept pets, but you have a much better choice today than even a few years ago. To find a dog-friendly lodging, look at *On the Road Again With Man's Best Friend*, a series of directories that detail bed and breakfasts, inns, family resorts and other hotels/motels. Some places require a refundable deposit to cover any damage incurred by the dog. More B&Bs accept pets now, but some restrict the size.

If taking Rufus with you is not feasible, check out boarding kennels in your area. Your veterinarian may offer this service, or recommend a kennel or two he or she is familiar with. Go see the facilities for yourself, ask about exercise, diet, housing, and so on. Or, if you'd rather have Rufus stay home, look into bonded petsitters, many of whom will also bring in the mail and water your plants.

chapter 11

Your Dog
and your
Community

by Bardi McLennan

Step outside your home with your dog and you are no longer just family, you are both part of your community. This is when the phrase "responsible pet ownership" takes on serious implications. For starters, it means you pick up after your dog—not just occasionally, but every time your dog eliminates away from home. That means you have joined the Plastic Baggy Brigade! You always have plastic sandwich bags in your pocket and several in the car. It means you teach your kids how to use them, too. If you think this is "yucky," just imagine what

the person (a non-doggy person) who inadvertently steps in the mess thinks!

Your responsibility extends to your neighbors: To their ears (no annoying barking); to their property (their garbage, their lawn, their flower beds, their cat— especially their cat); to their kids (on bikes, at play); to their kids' toys and sports equipment.

There are numerous dog-related laws, ranging from simple dog licensing and leash laws to those holding you liable for any physical injury or property damage done by your dog. These laws are in place to protect everyone in the community, including you and your dog. There are town ordinances and state laws which are by no means the same in all towns or all states. Ignorance of the law won't get you off the hook. The time to find out what the laws are where you live is now.

Be sure your dog's license is current. This is not just a good local ordinance, it can make the difference between finding your lost dog or not.

Dressing your dog up makes him appealing to strangers.

Many states now require proof of rabies vaccination and that the dog has been spayed or neutered before issuing a license. At the same time, keep up the dog's annual immunizations.

Never let your dog run loose in the neighborhood. This will not only keep you on the right side of the leash law, it's the outdoor version of the rule about not giving your dog "freedom to get into trouble."

Good Canine Citizen

Sometimes it's hard for a dog's owner to assess whether or not the dog is sufficiently socialized to be accepted by the community at large. Does Rufus or Rufina display good, controlled behavior in public? The AKC's Canine Good Citizen program is available through many dog organizations. If your dog passes the test, the title "CGC" is earned.

The overall purpose is to turn your dog into a good neighbor and to teach you about your responsibility to your community as a dog owner. Here are the ten things your dog must do willingly:

1. Accept a stranger stopping to chat with you.
2. Sit and be petted by a stranger.
3. Allow a stranger to handle him or her as a groomer or veterinarian would.
4. Walk nicely on a loose lead.
5. Walk calmly through a crowd.
6. Sit and down on command, then stay in a sit or down position while you walk away.
7. Come when called.
8. Casually greet another dog.
9. React confidently to distractions.
10. Accept being left alone with someone other than you and not become overly agitated or nervous.

Schools and Dogs

Schools are getting involved with pet ownership on an educational level. It has been proven that children who are kind to animals are humane in their attitude toward other people as adults.

A dog is a child's best friend, and so children are often primary pet owners, if not the primary caregivers. Unfortunately, they are also the ones most often bitten by dogs. This occurs due to a lack of understanding that pets, no matter how sweet, cuddly and loving, are still animals. Schools, along with parents, dog clubs, dog fanciers and the AKC, are working to change all that with video programs for children not only in grade school, but in the nursery school and pre-kindergarten age group. Teaching youngsters how to be responsible dog owners is important community work. When your dog has a CGC, volunteer to take part in an educational classroom event put on by your dog club.

Boy Scout Merit Badge

A Merit Badge for Dog Care can be earned by any Boy Scout ages 11 to 18. The requirements are not easy, but amount to a complete course in responsible dog care and general ownership. Here are just a few of the things a Scout must do to earn that badge:

> Point out ten parts of the dog using the correct names.
>
> Give a report (signed by parent or guardian) on your care of the dog (feeding, food used, housing, exercising, grooming and bathing), plus what has been done to keep the dog healthy.
>
> Explain the right way to obedience train a dog, and demonstrate three comments.
>
> Several of the requirements have to do with health care, including first aid, handling a hurt dog, and the dangers of home treatment for a serious ailment.
>
> The final requirement is to know the local laws and ordinances involving dogs.

There are similar programs for Girl Scouts and 4-H members.

Local Clubs

Local dog clubs are no longer in existence just to put on a yearly dog show. Today, they are apt to be the hub of the community's involvement with pets. Dog clubs conduct educational forums with big-name speakers, stage demonstrations of canine talent in a busy mall and take dogs of various breeds to schools for classroom discussion.

The quickest way to feel accepted as a member in a club is to volunteer your services! Offer to help with something—anything—and watch your popularity (and your interest) grow.

Therapy Dogs

Once your dog has earned that essential CGC and reliably demonstrates a steady, calm temperament, you could look into what therapy dogs are doing in your area.

Therapy dogs go with their owners to visit patients at hospitals or nursing homes, generally remaining on leash but able to coax a pat from a stiffened hand, a smile from a blank face, a few words from sealed lips or a hug from someone in need of love.

Your dog can make a difference in lots of lives.

Nursing homes cover a wide range of patient care. Some specialize in care of the elderly, some in the treatment of specific illnesses, some in physical therapy. Children's facilities also welcome visits from trained therapy dogs for boosting morale in their pediatric patients. Hospice care for the terminally ill and the at-home care of AIDS patients are other areas where this canine visiting is desperately needed. Therapy dog training comes first.

There is a lot more involved than just taking your nice friendly pooch to someone's bedside. Doing therapy dog work involves your own emotional stability as well as that of your dog. But once you have met all the requirements for this work, making the rounds once a week or once a month with your therapy dog is possibly the most rewarding of all community activities.

Disaster Aid

This community service is definitely not for everyone, partly because it is time-consuming. The initial training is rigorous, and there can be no let-up in the continuing workouts, because members are on call 24 hours a day to go wherever they are needed at a moment's notice. But if you think you would like to be able to assist in a disaster, look into search-and-rescue work. The network of search-and-rescue volunteers is worldwide, and all members of the American Rescue Dog Association (ARDA) who are qualified to do this work are volunteers who train and maintain their own dogs.

Physical Aid

Most people are familiar with Seeing Eye dogs, which serve as blind people's eyes, but not with all the other work that dogs are trained to do to assist the disabled. Dogs are also specially trained to pull wheelchairs, carry school books, pick up dropped objects, open and close doors. Some also are ears for the deaf. All these assistance-trained dogs, by the way, are allowed anywhere "No Pet" signs exist (as are therapy dogs when

properly identified). Getting started in any of this fascinating work requires a background in dog training and canine behavior, but there are also volunteer jobs ranging from answering the phone to cleaning out kennels to providing a foster home for a puppy. You have only to ask.

Making the rounds with your therapy dog can be very rewarding.

part four

Beyond the

Basics

chapter 12

Recommended Reading

Books

ABOUT HEALTH CARE

Ackerman, Lowell. *Guide to Skin and Haircoat Problems in Dogs.* Loveland, Colo.: Alpine Publications, 1994.

Alderton, David. *The Dog Care Manual.* Hauppauge, N.Y.: Barron's Educational Series, Inc., 1986.

American Kennel Club. *American Kennel Club Dog Care and Training.* New York: Howell Book House, 1991.

Bamberger, Michelle, DVM. *Help! The Quick Guide to First Aid for Your Dog.* New York: Howell Book House, 1995.

Carlson, Delbert, DVM, and James Giffin, MD. *Dog Owner's Home Veterinary Handbook.* New York: Howell Book House, 1992.

DeBitetto, James, DVM, and Sarah Hodgson. *You & Your Puppy.* New York: Howell Book House, 1995.

Humphries, Jim, DVM. *Dr. Jim's Animal Clinic for Dogs.* New York: Howell Book House, 1994.

McGinnis, Terri. *The Well Dog Book.* New York: Random House, 1991.

Pitcairn, Richard and Susan. *Natural Health for Dogs.* Emmaus, Pa.: Rodale Press, 1982.

ABOUT DOG SHOWS

Hall, Lynn. *Dog Showing for Beginners.* New York: Howell Book House, 1994.

Nichols, Virginia Tuck. *How to Show Your Own Dog.* Neptune, N. J.: TFH, 1970.

Vanacore, Connie. *Dog Showing, An Owner's Guide.* New York: Howell Book House, 1990.

ABOUT TRAINING

Ammen, Amy. *Training in No Time*. New York: Howell Book House, 1995.

Baer, Ted. *Communicating With Your Dog*. Hauppauge, N.Y.: Barron's Educational Series, Inc., 1989.

Benjamin, Carol Lea. *Dog Problems*. New York: Howell Book House, 1989.

Benjamin, Carol Lea. *Dog Training for Kids*. New York: Howell Book House, 1988.

Benjamin, Carol Lea. *Mother Knows Best*. New York: Howell Book House, 1985.

Benjamin, Carol Lea. *Surviving Your Dog's Adolescence*. New York: Howell Book House, 1993.

Bohnenkamp, Gwen. *Manners for the Modern Dog*. San Francisco: Perfect Paws, 1990.

Dibra, Bashkim. *Dog Training by Bash*. New York: Dell, 1992.

Dunbar, Ian, PhD, MRCVS. *Dr. Dunbar's Good Little Dog Book*, James & Kenneth Publishers, 2140 Shattuck Ave. #2406, Berkeley, Calif. 94704. (510) 658–8588. Order from the publisher.

Dunbar, Ian, PhD, MRCVS. *How to Teach a New Dog Old Tricks*, James & Kenneth Publishers. Order from the publisher; address above.

Dunbar, Ian, PhD, MRCVS, and Gwen Bohnenkamp. Booklets on *Preventing Aggression; Housetraining; Chewing; Digging; Barking; Socialization; Fearfulness; and Fighting*, James & Kenneth Publishers. Order from the publisher; address above.

Evans, Job Michael. *People, Pooches and Problems*. New York: Howell Book House, 1991.

Kilcommons, Brian and Sarah Wilson. *Good Owners, Great Dogs*. New York: Warner Books, 1992.

McMains, Joel M. *Dog Logic—Companion Obedience*. New York: Howell Book House, 1992.

Rutherford, Clarice and David H. Neil, MRCVS. *How to Raise a Puppy You Can Live With*. Loveland, Colo.: Alpine Publications, 1982.

Volhard, Jack and Melissa Bartlett. *What All Good Dogs Should Know: The Sensible Way to Train*. New York: Howell Book House, 1991.

ABOUT BREEDING

Harris, Beth J. Finder. *Breeding a Litter, The Complete Book of Prenatal and Postnatal Care*. New York: Howell Book House, 1983.

Holst, Phyllis, DVM. *Canine Reproduction*. Loveland, Colo.: Alpine Publications, 1985.

Walkowicz, Chris and Bonnie Wilcox, DVM. *Successful Dog Breeding, The Complete Handbook of Canine Midwifery*. New York: Howell Book House, 1994.

ABOUT ACTIVITIES

American Rescue Dog Association. *Search and Rescue Dogs*. New York: Howell Book House, 1991.

Barwig, Susan and Stewart Hilliard. *Schutzhund*. New York: Howell Book House, 1991.

Beaman, Arthur S. *Lure Coursing*. New York: Howell Book House, 1994.

Daniels, Julie. *Enjoying Dog Agility—From Backyard to Competition*. New York: Doral Publishing, 1990.

Davis, Kathy Diamond. *Therapy Dogs*. New York: Howell Book House, 1992.

Gallup, Davis Anne. *Running With Man's Best Friend*. Loveland, Colo.: Alpine Publications, 1986.

Habgood, Dawn and Robert. *On the Road Again With Man's Best Friend*. New England, Mid-Atlantic, West Coast and Southeast editions. Selective guides to area bed and breakfasts, inns, hotels and resorts that welcome guests and their dogs. New York: Howell Book House, 1995.

Holland, Vergil S. *Herding Dogs*. New York: Howell Book House, 1994.

LaBelle, Charlene G. *Backpacking With Your Dog*. Loveland, Colo.: Alpine Publications, 1993.

Simmons-Moake, Jane. *Agility Training, The Fun Sport for All Dogs*. New York: Howell Book House, 1991.

Spencer, James B. *Hup! Training Flushing Spaniels the American Way*. New York: Howell Book House, 1992.

Spencer, James B. *Point! Training the All-Seasons Birddog*. New York: Howell Book House, 1995.

Tarrant, Bill. *Training the Hunting Retriever*. New York: Howell Book House, 1991.

Volhard, Jack and Wendy. *The Canine Good Citizen*. New York: Howell Book House, 1994.

General Titles

Haggerty, Captain Arthur J. *How to Get Your Pet Into Show Business*. New York: Howell Book House, 1994.

McLennan, Bardi. *Dogs and Kids, Parenting Tips*. New York: Howell Book House, 1993.

Moran, Patti J. *Pet Sitting for Profit, A Complete Manual for Professional Success*. New York: Howell Book House, 1992.

Scalisi, Danny and Libby Moses. *When Rover Just Won't Do, Over 2,000 Suggestions for Naming Your Dog.* New York: Howell Book House, 1993.

Sife, Wallace, PhD. *The Loss of a Pet.* New York: Howell Book House, 1993.

Wrede, Barbara J. *Civilizing Your Puppy.* Hauppauge, N.Y.: Barron's Educational Series, 1992.

Magazines

The AKC GAZETTE, The Official Journal for the Sport of Purebred Dogs. American Kennel Club, 51 Madison Ave., New York, NY.

Bloodlines Journal. United Kennel Club, 100 E. Kilgore Rd., Kalamazoo, MI.

Dog Fancy. Fancy Publications, 3 Burroughs, Irvine, CA 92718

Dog World. Maclean Hunter Publishing Corp., 29 N. Wacker Dr., Chicago, IL 60606.

Videos

"SIRIUS Puppy Training," by Ian Dunbar, PhD, MRCVS. James & Kenneth Publishers, 2140 Shattuck Ave. #2406, Berkeley, CA 94704. Order from the publisher.

"Training the Companion Dog," from Dr. Dunbar's British TV Series, James & Kenneth Publishers. (See address above).

The American Kennel Club produces videos on every breed of dog, as well as on hunting tests, field trials and other areas of interest to purebred dog owners. For more information, write to AKC/Video Fulfillment, 5580 Centerview Dr., Suite 200, Raleigh, NC 27606.

chapter 13

Resources

Breed Clubs

Every breed recognized by the American Kennel Club has a national (parent) club. National clubs are a great source of information on your breed. You can get the name of the secretary of the club by contacting:

The American Kennel Club
51 Madison Avenue
New York, NY 10010
(212) 696-8200

There are also numerous all-breed, individual breed, obedience, hunting and other special-interest dog clubs across the country. The American Kennel Club can provide you with a geographical list of clubs to find ones in your area. Contact them at the above address.

Registry Organizations

Registry organizations register purebred dogs. The American Kennel Club is the oldest and largest in this country, and currently recognizes over 130 breeds. The United Kennel Club registers some breeds the AKC doesn't (including the American Pit Bull Terrier and the Miniature Fox Terrier) as well as many of the same breeds. The others included here are for your reference; the AKC can provide you with a list of foreign registries.

American Kennel Club
51 Madison Avenue
New York, NY 10010

United Kennel Club (UKC)
100 E. Kilgore Road
Kalamazoo, MI 49001-5598

American Dog Breeders Assn.
P.O. Box 1771
Salt Lake City, UT 84110
(Registers American Pit Bull Terriers)

Canadian Kennel Club
89 Skyway Avenue
Etobicoke, Ontario
Canada M9W 6R4

National Stock Dog Registry
P.O. Box 402
Butler, IN 46721
(Registers working stock dogs)

Orthopedic Foundation for Animals (OFA)
2300 E. Nifong Blvd.
Columbia, MO 65201-3856
(Hip registry)

Activity Clubs

Write to these organizations for information on the
activities they sponsor.

American Kennel Club
51 Madison Avenue
New York, NY 10010
(Conformation Shows, Obedience Trials, Field
Trials and Hunting Tests, Agility, Canine Good

Citizen, Lure Coursing, Herding, Tracking,
Earthdog Tests, Coonhunting.)

United Kennel Club
100 E. Kilgore Road
Kalamazoo, MI 49001-5598
(Conformation Shows, Obedience Trials, Agility,
Hunting for Various Breeds, Terrier Trials and
more.)

North American Flyball Assn.
1342 Jeff St.
Ypsilanti, MI 48198

International Sled Dog Racing Assn.
P.O. Box 446
Norman, ID 83848-0446

North American Working Dog Assn., Inc.
Southeast Kreisgruppe
P.O. Box 833
Brunswick, GA 31521

Trainers

Association of Pet Dog Trainers
P.O. Box 385
Davis, CA 95617
(800) PET–DOGS

American Dog Trainers' Network
161 West 4th St.
New York, NY 10014
(212) 727–7257

**National Association of Dog Obedience
Instructors**
2286 East Steel Rd.
St. Johns, MI 48879

Associations

American Dog Owners Assn.
1654 Columbia Tpk.
Castleton, NY 12033
(Combats anti-dog legislation)

Delta Society
P.O. Box 1080
Renton, WA 98057-1080
(Promotes the human/animal bond through
pet-assisted therapy and other programs)

Dog Writers Assn. of America (DWAA)
Sally Cooper, Secy.
222 Woodchuck Ln.
Harwinton, CT 06791

National Assn. for Search and Rescue (NASAR)
P.O. Box 3709
Fairfax, VA 22038

Therapy Dogs International
6 Hilltop Road
Mendham, NJ 07945